1001 ESSENTIAL SENTENCES
FOR ELEMENTARY ENGLISH LEARNERS

CEDU 쎄듀는 A **C**omprehensive **E**nglish e**DU**cation(종합적 영어교육)의 약자입니다.

펴낸이	김기훈 · 김진희
펴낸곳	(주)쎄듀 / 서울시 강남구 논현로 305 (역삼동)
발행일	2016년 11월 21일 초판 1쇄
내용문의	www.cedubook.com
구입문의	콘텐츠 마케팅 사업본부
	Tel. 02-6241-2007
	Fax. 02-2058-0209
등록번호	제 22-2472호
ISBN	978-89-6806-077-9

천일문 sentence

세이펜과
초등코치 천일문 Sentence의 만남!

✦ ✦ ✦

〈초등코치 천일문 Sentence〉는 세이펜이 적용된 도서입니다.
세이펜을 영어에 가져다 대기만 하면 원어민이 들려주는 생생한 영어 발음과
억양을 바로 확인할 수 있습니다.

*세이펜은 본 교재에 포함되어 있지 않습니다.
기존에 보유하신 세이펜이 있다면 핀파일만 다운로드해서 바로 이용하실 수 있습니다.
단, Role-Play 기능은 SBS-1000 이후 모델에서만 구동됩니다.

초등코치 천일문 시리즈
with 세이펜

원어민 음성 실시간 반복학습	녹음 기능으로 쉐도잉 발음교정	게임 기능으로 재미있고 유익하게	Role-Play로 자신감까지 Up

초등코치 천일문 시리즈 Sentence 1권~5권, Grammar 1권~3권, Voca&Story 1권~2권 모두
세이펜을 활용하여 원어민 MP3 음성 재생 서비스를 이용할 수 있습니다.

(책 앞면 하단에 세이펜 로고 **SAYPEN TV** 가 있습니다.)

세이펜 핀파일 다운로드 안내

STEP ① 세이펜과 컴퓨터를 USB 케이블로 연결하세요.

STEP ② 쎄듀북 홈페이지(www.cedubook.com)에 접속 후, 학습자료실 메뉴에서 학습할 교재를 찾아 이동합니다.

> 초·중등교재 ▶ 구문 ▶ 학습교재 클릭 ▶ 세이펜 핀파일 자료 클릭
> ▶ 다운로드 (저장을 '다른 이름으로 저장'으로 변경하여 저장소를 USB로 변경) ▶ 완료

STEP ③ 음원 다운로드가 완료되면 세이펜과 컴퓨터의 USB 케이블을 분리하세요.

STEP ④ 세이펜을 분리하면 "시스템을 초기화 중입니다. 잠시만 기다려 주세요" 라는 멘트가 나옵니다.

STEP ⑤ 멘트 종료 후 세이펜을 〈초등코치 천일문 Sentence〉 표지의 제목 부분에 대보세요.
효과음이 나온 후 바로 학습을 시작할 수 있습니다.

참고사항

◆ 세이펜에서 제작된 모든 기종(기존에 보유하고 계신 기종도 호환 가능)으로 사용이 가능합니다. 단, Sentence 교재의 Role-Play 기능은
레인보우 SBS-1000 기종에서만 구동됩니다. (신규 구매자는 SBS-1000 이후 모델의 구매를 권장합니다.)

◆ 모든 기종은 세이펜에서 권장하는 최신 펌웨어 업데이트를 진행해 주시기 바랍니다.
업데이트는 세이펜 홈페이지(www.saypen.com)에서 가능합니다.

◆ 초등코치 천일문 시리즈의 핀파일은 쎄듀북 홈페이지(www.cedubook.com)와 세이펜 홈페이지(www.saypen.com)에서
모두 다운로드 가능합니다.

◆ 세이펜을 이용하지 않는 학습자는 쎄듀북 홈페이지 부가학습자료, 교재 내 QR코드 이미지 등을 활용하여 원어민 음성으로
학습하실 수 있습니다.

◆ 기타 문의사항은 www.cedubook.com / 02-3272-4766으로 연락 바랍니다.

천일문
sentence

✦ ✦ ✦

2

저자

김기훈　現 ㈜ 쎄듀 대표이사
　　　　現 메가스터디 영어영역 대표강사
　　　　前 서울특별시 교육청 외국어 교육정책자문위원회 위원
　　저서　천일문 / 천일문 Training Book / 천일문 GRAMMAR / 초등코치 천일문
　　　　　어법끝 / 어휘끝 / 첫단추 / 쎈쓰업 / 파워업 / 빈칸백서 / 오답백서
　　　　　쎄듀 본영어 / 문법의 골든룰 101 / ALL씀 서술형 / 수능실감
　　　　　거침없이 Writing / Grammar Q / Reading Q / Listening Q
　　　　　왓츠 그래머 / 왓츠 리딩 / 패턴으로 말하는 초등 필수 영단어 등

쎄듀 영어교육연구센터
쎄듀 영어교육센터는 영어 콘텐츠에 대한 전문지식과 경험을 바탕으로
최고의 교육 콘텐츠를 만들고자 최선의 노력을 다하는 전문가 집단입니다.
인지영 책임연구원 · **장혜승** 선임연구원

검토위원

성윤선　現 Charles G. Emery Elementary School 교사
　　약력　하버드대학교 교육대학원 Language and Literacy 석사
　　　　　이화여자대학교 교육공학, 영어교육 복수 전공
　　　　　가톨릭대학교 교수학습센터 연구원
　　　　　이화여자대학교 교수학습개발원 연구원
　　　　　한국교육개발원 연구원

마케팅　　　콘텐츠 마케팅 사업본부
영업　　　　문병구
제작　　　　정승호
인디자인 편집　올댓에디팅
표지 디자인　윤혜영
내지 디자인　에피그램
영문교열　　Eric Scheusner

Foreword

〈초등코치 천일문 SENTENCE〉 시리즈를 펴내며

초등 영어, 무엇을 어떻게 시작해야 할까요?

자녀에게 영어 공부를 시키는 목적은 여러 가지일 것입니다. '우리 아이가 원어민처럼 영어를 잘했으면 좋겠다', '생활하는 데 영어가 걸림돌이 되지 않으면 좋겠다'라는 바람에서, 또는 중학교 내신이나 대학 입시를 위해 영어 공부를 시키기도 하지요.

영어를 공부하는 목표가 무엇이 되든, 영어의 기초가 잡혀 있지 않으면 새로운 것을 배우는 데 시간과 노력이 더 많이 들 수밖에 없습니다. 그리고 영어는 아이가 공부해야 하는 단 하나의 과목이 아니기에, 영어 공부에 비교적 많은 시간을 투자할 수 있는 초등학생 시기가 매우 중요하지요.

〈초등코치 천일문 SENTENCE〉 시리즈는 기초를 세우기에 가장 적절한 초등학생 시기에 **1,001개 통문장 암기로 영어의 기초를 완성**할 수 있도록 기획되었습니다. 1,001개 문장은 꼭 알아야 할 패턴 112개와 실생활에 유용한 표현들로 구성되었습니다.

| 문장과 덩어리 표현(chunk)이 학습의 주가 됩니다.

영어를 학습할 때는 문장(full sentence)과 덩어리 표현(chunk) 학습법이 더욱 효과적입니다. 〈초등코치 천일문 SENTENCE〉는 우리말 설명을 최소화하고 문장 자체에 집중할 수 있도록 구성했습니다. 책에 수록된 모든 문장과 표현, 대화는 現 미국 공립 초등학교 선생님의 검토를 받아 완성되었습니다.

| 문장 암기를 쉽게 할 수 있도록 설계했습니다.

문장과 표현이 자연스럽게 7번 반복되어 책을 따라 하다 보면 자동으로 1,001개 문장을 암기할 수 있습니다. 그리고 이해와 기억을 돕기 위해 재미있는 그림으로 새로운 표현들과 상황을 제시했습니다. 또한, 대부분 문장의 주어를 '나(I)'로 하여 아이들이 실생활에서도 자주 말하고 쓸 수 있도록 했습니다.

1,001개 통문장 암기로 탄탄한 기초가 세워지면, 내신, 수능, 말하기·듣기 등 앞으로의 모든 영어 학습에 대한 불안감이 해소될 것입니다. 〈초등코치 천일문 SENTENCE〉 시리즈와의 만남을 통해 영어 학습이 더욱더 쉬워지고 즐거워지는 경험을 꼭 할 수 있기를 희망합니다.

저 자

추천의 글

외국어 학습은 수년의 시간이 수반되는 장거리 경주입니다. 따라서, 잘못된 방식으로 학습을 시작해 외국어 학습의 즐거움을 초반에 잃어버리면, 끝까지 지속하지 못하고 중도에 포기하게 됩니다. 쎄듀의 초등코치 천일문은 대한민국의 초등 영어 학습자들이 효과적이고 효율적으로 영어학습의 경주를 시작할 수 있도록 여러분의 걸음을 친절하고 꼼꼼하게 안내해 줍니다.

효과적인 초등 영어 학습을 약속합니다.

영어 학습 과정에서 단어를 하나하나 익히는 것도 물론 중요하지만, 덩어리(chunk) 또는 패턴으로 다양한 영어 표현을 익히면 영어를 보다 유창하게 구사하고, 빠른 속도로 이해할 수 있습니다. 쎄듀의 초등코치 천일문은 일상 생활에서 가장 빈번히 사용되는 112개의 문장 패턴을 담았습니다.

또한, 각 문장 패턴당 8~9개의 훈련 문장들과 함께 4개의 짧은 대화가 수록되어 해당 패턴을 실제로 어떻게 사용할 수 있는지 보여줍니다. 이렇게 다양한 예문과 구체적인 대화 상황을 제시함으로써 쎄듀 초등코치 천일문은 언어 학습에 필수적인 패턴을 활용한 반복 학습을 이루어 갑니다.

112개의 필수 영어 문장 패턴과 이를 활용한 1,001개의 예문 학습, 그리고 구석구석 꼼꼼하게 안내된 어휘 학습까지. 쎄듀의 초등코치 천일문은 영어 학습을 시작하는 학생들이 탄탄한 영어의 기초를 다질 수 있는 효과적인 학습방법을 제시합니다.

효율적인 초등 영어 학습을 약속합니다.

애써 영어 공부를 했는데, 실제 영어를 사용하는 현장에서 활용할 수 없다면 어떻게 해야 할까요? 기존의 학습 내용을 지우고, 출발점으로 돌아가 다시 시작해야 합니다. 장거리를 달려야 하는데 다시 시작이라니 지칠 수밖에 없습니다.

쎄듀의 초등코치 천일문은 한 문장 한 문장, 대화 하나하나를 미국 초등학생들이 실제로 사용하는지 철저히 고려하여 엄선된 내용을 채택하였습니다. 초등학생들의 관심 주제를 바탕으로 문장과 대화들이 작성되어 학습자 모두 내용을 친숙하게 느낄 수 있습니다.

친숙한 대화 소재를 바탕으로 한 실제적인 영어 예문 학습을 통해, 본 교재를 이용한 학생들은 잘못된 공부로 인한 소진 없이 효율적으로 영어의 기본기를 다질 수 있습니다.

LA에서, 성윤선

Series

1권 Track 01~24 001~212	2권 Track 25~48 213~428	3권 Track 49~70 429~624	4권 Track 71~91 625~813	5권 Track 92~112 814~1001
This is ~.	I can ~.	I'm going to ~.	I started -ing.	Give me ~.
That's ~.	I can't ~.	He[She]'s going to ~.	I began to ~.	He[She] gave me ~.
I am a/an ~.	You can ~.	Are you going to ~?	Stop -ing.	I'll show you ~.
I am ~.	Can I ~?	I was about to ~.	I[We] kept -ing.	I'll tell you ~.
I'm not ~.	Can you ~?	I'm -ing.	I want to ~.	It makes me ~.
You are ~.	I[You] should ~.	He[She]'s -ing.	I don't want to ~.	He[She, It] made me ~.
He[She] is ~.	You must ~.	Are you -ing?	I wanted to ~.	Let me ~.
He[She] is in ~.	I[You] might ~.	I was -ing.	I like to ~.	Help me ~.
It is ~.	I have to ~.	What's ~?	I need to ~.	I want you to ~.
Are you ~?	You have to ~.	What do you ~?	I tried to ~.	I saw him[her] -ing.
It's ~.	You don't have to ~.	What are you -ing?	I'm supposed to ~.	I heard him[her] -ing.
There is ~.	I had to ~.	Who is ~?	It's time to ~.	I think (that) ~.
There are ~.	I used to ~.	Why do you ~?	Do you know how to ~?	I don't think (that) ~.
Is[Are] there any ~?	I was ~.	Why don't we ~?	I don't know what to ~.	I thought (that) ~.
There's no ~.	He[She] was ~.	Where is ~?	He[She] seems to ~.	I know (that) ~.
I have ~.	I went to ~.	Where did you ~?	You look ~.	I knew (that) ~.
He[She] has ~.	I put it ~.	How do you ~?	I feel ~.	I don't know what ~.
I want ~.	I didn't ~.	When are you going to ~?	I got ~.	I guess (that) ~.
I like ~.	Did you ~?	What a[an]-!	I'm getting ~.	I hope (that) ~.
I hate ~.	I[We] will ~.	Do[Be] ~.	He[She] seems ~.	I'm sure (that) ~.
I need ~.	He[She] will ~.	Don't ~.	It looks like ~.	That's why ~.
I don't ~.	I won't ~.	Let's ~.		
Do you ~?	I'll be able to ~.			
Does he[she] ~?	Will you ~?			

Preview

Step 1

대표 문장과 패턴을 확인합니다.

미국 도서관 협회 추천 영어 동화책을 분석하여 가장 많이 쓰이는 패턴 112가지를 쉽고 간략한 설명과 함께 여러 예문으로 제시했습니다.

QR코드

휴대폰을 통해 QR코드를 인식하면, 본문의 모든 문장, 단어 및 청크, 대화의 MP3 파일이 재생됩니다.

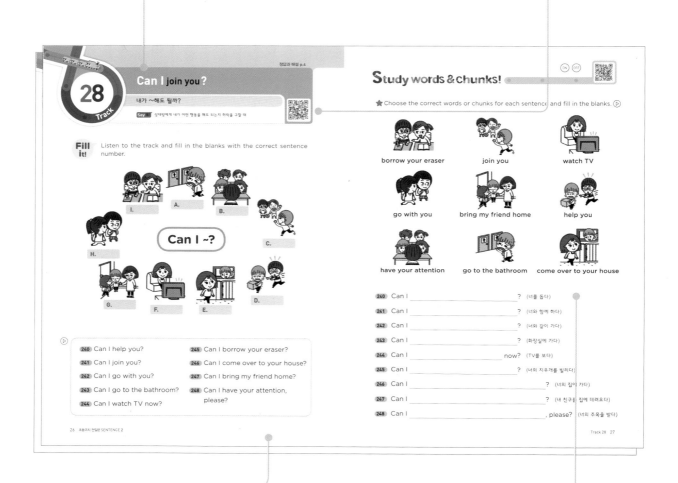

Step 2

미국 현지 초등학생 원어민 성우들이 읽는 문장들을 듣고 그림과 연결합니다.

귀로 듣고 눈으로 보면서 직접 패턴과 청크들을 연결합니다. 보기와 듣기까지 동시에 함으로써 학습 내용을 오래 기억할 수 있습니다.

Step 3

단어와 청크를 집중적으로 연습합니다.

단어와 청크 뜻에 맞는 그림을 연결해 보면서 문장을 완성합니다. 실생활에서 자주 쓸 수 있는 유용한 표현들을 익힐 수 있습니다.

각 그림 상황에 알맞은 문장을 완성합니다.

앞에서 배운 패턴과 청크를 사용하여 완전한 문장을 써 봅니다. 재미 있는 그림을 통해 문장이 실제로 사용되는 상황을 알 수 있습니다.

각 대화 상황에 알맞은 문장을 넣어 봅니다.

학습한 문장이 실제로 어떤 대화 상황에서 쓰일 수 있는지 확실하게 알 수 있습니다.

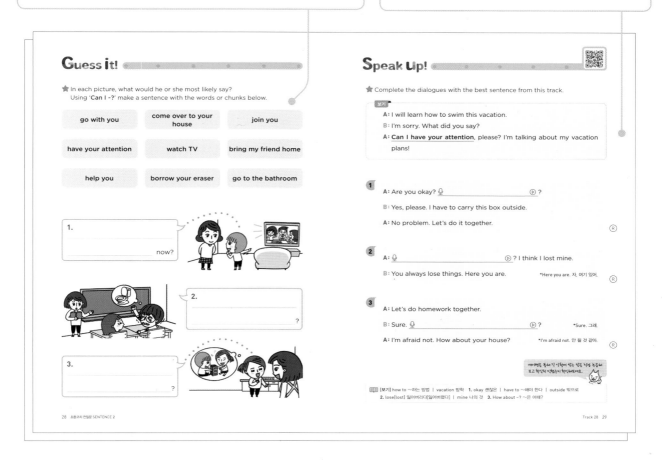

워크북으로 단어 및 청크, 문장을 마스터합니다.

무료 부가서비스 자료로 완벽하게 복습합니다.

1. 어휘리스트   2. 어휘테스트   3. 본문 해석 연습지
4. 본문 말하기·영작 연습지   5. MP3 파일

* 모든 자료는 www.cedubook.com에서 다운로드 가능합니다.

MP3 활용하기

〈초등코치 천일문 SENTENCE〉 부가서비스 자료에는 본문의 모든 문장, 단어 및 청크, 대화의 MP3 파일이 들어 있습니다.

· 미국 현지 초등학생 원어민 성우의 생생하고 정확한 발음과 억양을 확인할 수 있습니다.

· 문장은 2회씩 녹음되어 있습니다.

Strong Points

1 20일 또는 16일 완성

〈초등코치 천일문 SENTENCE〉 시리즈는 한 권을 20일 또는 16일 동안 학습할 수 있도록 구성되어 있습니다. 아이의 상황에 맞게 계획표를 선택하여 학습할 수 있습니다.

2 복잡한 문법 설명 없이도 가능한 학습

어렵고 복잡한 문법 용어를 설명할 필요가 없습니다. 패턴과 문장 자체의 의미를 받아들이는 데 집중하도록 구성되어 부담 없이 학습해 나갈 수 있습니다.

3 문장이 자연스럽게 외워지는 자동 암기 시스템

각 트랙에는 8~9개의 문장이 수록되어 있습니다. 본책과 워크북에는 이러한 문장들과 문장 속 표현들이 7번이나 자연스럽게 반복되는 효과가 있어서 책을 따라 하다 보면 자동적으로 암기가 가능합니다.

★ MP3 파일을 반복해서 들으면 암기에 더욱 효과적입니다.
책에 실린 모든 문장은 초등학생 원어민 성우 Arthur와 Claire가 미국 현지에서 녹음했습니다.

🖊 세이펜으로 더 쉽게, 더 자주 반복해서 들을 수 있습니다.
또한, Study words & chunks의 게임 기능을 통해 더욱 재미있게 암기할 수 있습니다.

4 이해와 기억을 돕는 1,337개의 그림

그림과 상황을 통해 문장의 의미를 직관적으로 이해할 수 있도록 1,001개의 표현을 묘사한 그림과 336개의 대화 상황을 나타내는 그림을 실었습니다.

my mistake

5 또래 원어민 친구와 나눠보는 대화

각 트랙의 마지막 페이지에는 학습한 문장을 채워볼 수 있는 dialogue 4개가 실려 있습니다. 이 대화는 모두 뉴욕에 거주하는 초등학생 원어민 성우 Eden과 Kara가 미국 현지에서 녹음한 것으로, A와 B 중 골라서 role playing을 할 수 있습니다. 꾸준히 연습하다 보면, 실제로 원어민 친구를 만나도 당황하지 않고 자연스럽게 대화할 수 있습니다.

세이펜의 Role-Play 기능을 활용하여 더욱 생생한 대화를 경험해 볼 수 있습니다. 세이펜으로 각 dialogue의 빈칸을 포함한 문장 전체를 녹음한 후 Role-Play 버튼 Ⓡ에 대면, 녹음한 문장이 원어민의 대화와 함께 자연스럽게 재생됩니다.

6 다양한 부가 학습 자료로 완벽 복습

1,001개의 문장을 다양한 부가 학습 자료로 완벽하게 복습할 수 있습니다. 테스트 자료로도 유용하게 활용하실 수 있습니다.
(www.cedubook.com에서 무료로 다운로드 가능합니다.)

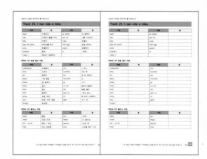

어휘리스트 & 어휘테스트
본문에 실린 모든 어휘를 학습할 수 있습니다. 어휘리스트로 학습한 후에는 어휘테스트로 어휘 실력을 점검해볼 수 있습니다.

본문 해석 연습지
1,001개 문장의 해석을 써보며 의미를 복습할 수 있습니다.

본문 말하기·영작 연습지
우리말 해석을 보고 영어로 바꿔 말하거나 써볼 수 있습니다.
말하기·영작 연습지는 '우리말 뜻을 보고 빈칸 채우기 ▶ 순서대로 어휘 배열하기 ▶ 뜻을 보며 영작하기'의 순서로 구성되어 있습니다.

Contents 📖

〈초등코치 천일문 SENTENCE 2〉 목차

책속책 **WORKBOOK** | 정답과 해설

Study Plan

<초등코치 천일문 SENTENCE 2> 학습 계획표

⭐ **20일 완성!**

	Track	공부한 날짜	
1일차	Track 25, 워크북/Track 26, 워크북	월	일
2일차	Track 27, 워크북/Track 28, 워크북	월	일
3일차	Track 29, 워크북/Track 30, 워크북	월	일
4일차	Track 31, 워크북/Track 32, 워크북	월	일
5일차	Track 33, 워크북/Track 34, 워크북	월	일
6일차	Track 25~27 Review	월	일
7일차	Track 28~30 Review	월	일
8일차	Track 31~34 Review	월	일
9일차	Track 35, 워크북/Track 36, 워크북	월	일
10일차	Track 37, 워크북/Track 38, 워크북	월	일
11일차	Track 39, 워크북/Track 40, 워크북	월	일
12일차	Track 41, 워크북/Track 42, 워크북	월	일
13일차	Track 43, 워크북/Track 44, 워크북	월	일
14일차	Track 35~37 Review	월	일
15일차	Track 38~40 Review	월	일
16일차	Track 41~44 Review	월	일
17일차	Track 45, 워크북/Track 46, 워크북	월	일
18일차	Track 47, 워크북/Track 48, 워크북	월	일
19일차	Track 45~46 Review	월	일
20일차	Track 47~48 Review	월	일

★ 16일 완성!

	Track	공부한 날짜	
1일차	Track 25~27, 워크북	월	일
2일차	Track 25~27 Review	월	일
3일차	Track 28~30, 워크북	월	일
4일차	Track 28~30 Review	월	일
5일차	Track 31~33, 워크북	월	일
6일차	Track 31~33 Review	월	일
7일차	Track 34~36, 워크북	월	일
8일차	Track 34~36 Review	월	일
9일차	Track 37~39, 워크북	월	일
10일차	Track 37~39 Review	월	일
11일차	Track 40~42, 워크북	월	일
12일차	Track 40~42 Review	월	일
13일차	Track 43~45, 워크북	월	일
14일차	Track 43~45 Review	월	일
15일차	Track 46~48, 워크북	월	일
16일차	Track 46~48 Review	월	일

Let's Start!

I can ride a bike.

나는 ~할 수 있어.

Say It! 내가 할 수 있는 것을 말할 때

Fill it! Listen to the track and fill in the blanks with the correct sentence number.

213 I can teach you.

214 I can ride a bike.

215 I can play the piano.

216 I can solve this problem.

217 I can make it.

218 I can do better.

219 I can wait for you.

220 I can make fried eggs.

221 I can explain it to you.

Study words & chunks!

⭐ Choose the correct words or chunks for each sentence and fill in the blanks. ▷

make fried eggs

teach you

make it

wait for you

explain it to you

play the piano

solve this problem

do better

ride a bike

213 I can _____. (너에게 가르쳐 주다)

214 I can _____. (자전거를 타다)

215 I can _____. (피아노를 치다)

216 I can _____. (이 문제를 해결하다)

217 I can _____. (해내다)

218 I can _____. (더 잘하다)

219 I can _____. (너를 기다리다)

220 I can _____. (달걀 프라이를 만들다)

221 I can _____. (너에게 그것을 설명하다)

Guess it!

⭐ In each picture, what would he or she most likely say?
Using 'I can ~.' make a sentence with the words or chunks below.

explain it to you	wait for you	ride a bike
make it	play the piano	make fried eggs
teach you	do better	solve this problem

1. _____

2. _____

3. _____

Speak Up!

⭐ Complete the dialogues with the best sentence from this track.

A: I can't understand this story. Can you tell me about it?

B: **I can explain it to you**. It's a story about a dream.

A: Really? I didn't know that.

1

A: Is there any food?

B: 🎤 _____ ▷. Do you want some?

A: Yes, please. I'm very hungry.

Ⓡ

2

A: We have one hundred meters to the top of the mountain.

B: 🎤 _____ ▷. I'm not tired at all.

A: Great! Let's go.

Ⓡ

3

A: You ran one hundred meters in 15 seconds. That's fast!

B: I want to try again. 🎤 _____ ▷.

A: Really? Okay. I'll time you.

Ⓡ

세이펜을 통해 각 상황에 맞는 말을 직접 녹음해
보고 확실히 익혔는지 확인해보세요.

📖 **[보기]** really 정말   **2.** meter (거리) 미터 ㅣ tired 지친, 피곤한 ㅣ not ~ at all 전혀 ~ 아닌 ㅣ let's ~하자
3. run[ran] 달리다[달렸다] ㅣ second (시간) 초 ㅣ want to ~하고 싶다 ㅣ time 시간을 재다

I can't believe it.

26
Track

나는 ~할 수 없어.

 Say It! 내가 할 수 없는 것이나 하지 못하는 것을 말할 때
*can't는 cannot(~할 수 없다)을 줄인 말이에요.

Fill it! Listen to the track and fill in the blanks with the correct sentence number.

222 I can't swim well.	**227** I can't find my glasses.
223 I can't go out now.	**228** I can't hear you.
224 I can't believe it.	**229** I can't remember his name.
225 I can't eat all this!	**230** I can't answer your question.
226 I can't talk about it.	

Study words & chunks!

⭐ Choose the correct words or chunks for each sentence and fill in the blanks. ▷

answer your question

talk about it

swim well

believe it

remember his name

find my glasses

go out

eat all this

hear you

222 I can't _____. (수영을 잘하다)

223 I can't _____ now. (나가다, 외출하다)

224 I can't _____. (그것을 믿다)

225 I can't _____ ! (이것을 다 먹다)

226 I can't _____. (그것에 대해 말하다)

227 I can't _____. (내 안경을 찾다)

228 I can't _____. (네 말을 듣다)

229 I can't _____. (그의 이름을 기억하다)

230 I can't _____. (너의 질문에 대답하다)

Guess it!

⭐ In each picture, what would he or she most likely say?
Using '**I can't ~.**' make a sentence with the words or chunks below.

find my glasses	remember his name	eat all this
believe it	talk about it	go out
swim well	answer your question	hear you

1. _____
   _____.

2. _____
   _____.

3. _____
   _____!

Speak Up!

⭐ Complete the dialogues with the best sentence from this track.

> 보기
>
> **A:** Come on. Let's go outside and play!
>
> **B: I can't go out** now. I have to finish my homework first.

1

A: Did you talk to the new student? What is his name?

B: 🎤 _____ ▷. But he was kind.

Ⓡ

2

A: 🎤 _____ ▷. Where are they?

B: I don't know. Did you check inside your bag?

Ⓡ

3

A: Did you hear that? It will be rainy on our picnic day.

B: Really? Are you sure? 🎤 _____ ▷.

A: I am sure. I saw it on the news.

Ⓡ

세이펜을 통해 각 상황에 맞는 말을 직접 녹음해 보고 확실히 익혔는지 확인해보세요.

📖 **[보기]** outside 밖으로 | have to ~해야 한다 | first 먼저 **2.** inside ~ 안쪽의, 속의 **3.** rainy 비가 오는 | sure 확실한 | see[saw] 보다[보았다]

You can go first.

27 Track

너는 ~해도 돼.

 Say It! 어떤 행동을 해도 된다고 허락하는 말을 할 때
*'너는 ~할 수 있어'라고 말할 때도 쓸 수 있어요.

Fill it! Listen to the track and fill in the blanks with the correct sentence number.

You can ~.

231 You can go home.	**236** You can ask me for help.
232 You can go first.	**237** You can have a seat here.
233 You can take it.	**238** You can share with me.
234 You can borrow my pencil.	**239** You can come over to my house.
235 You can play computer games.	

Study words & chunks!

⭐ Choose the correct words or chunks for each sentence and fill in the blanks. ▷

go first

share with me

play computer games

ask me for help

borrow my pencil

go home

take it

come over to my house

have a seat

231 You can _____. (집에 가다)

232 You can _____. (먼저 가다)

233 You can _____. (그것을 가져가다)

234 You can _____. (내 연필을 빌리다)

235 You can _____. (컴퓨터 게임을 하다)

236 You can _____. (나에게 도움을 요청하다)

237 You can _____ here. (자리에 앉다)

238 You can _____. (나와 함께 쓰다)

239 You can _____. (나의 집에 오다)

Guess it!

⭐ In each picture, what would he or she most likely say?
Using '**You can ~.**' make a sentence with the words or chunks below.

share with me	ask me for help	borrow my pencil
come over to my house	take it	go home
go first	play computer games	have a seat

1.

_____

_____ here.

2.

_____

_____ .

3.

_____

_____ .

Speak Up!

⭐ Complete the dialogues with the best sentence from this track.

> **보기**
>
> **A:** I have so much to do! I'll never finish.
>
> **B:** I'm not busy. **You can ask me for help**.
>
> **A:** Really? Thanks!

1

A: Let's play video games together!

B: Sounds great. 🎤 _____ ▷.

*Sounds great. 좋아.

A: Okay. It will be fun!

Ⓡ

2

A: I need to write something. But I don't have a pencil.

B: 🎤 _____ ▷. Here it is.

*Here it is. 자, 여기 있어.

Ⓡ

3

A: I have no time to wait in line.

B: 🎤 _____ ▷. I'm not in a hurry.

A: Thanks a lot!

Ⓡ

> 세이펜을 통해 각 상황에 맞는 말을 직접 녹음해
> 보고 확실히 익혔는지 확인해보세요.

📖 **[보기]** really 정말 **1.** video game 비디오 게임 **2.** need to ~해야 한다 | something 무엇 **3.** wait in line
줄을 서서 기다리다 | in a hurry 바쁜 | a lot 아주, 많이

Can I join you?

내가 ~해도 될까?

Say It! 상대방에게 내가 어떤 행동을 해도 되는지 허락을 구할 때

Fill it! Listen to the track and fill in the blanks with the correct sentence number.

Can I ~?

I.

A.

B.

C.

H.

G.

F.

E.

D.

240 Can I help you?

241 Can I join you?

242 Can I go with you?

243 Can I go to the bathroom?

244 Can I watch TV now?

245 Can I borrow your eraser?

246 Can I come over to your house?

247 Can I bring my friend home?

248 Can I have your attention, please?

Study words & chunks!

⭐ Choose the correct words or chunks for each sentence and fill in the blanks. ▷

borrow your eraser

join you

watch TV

go with you

bring my friend home

help you

have your attention

go to the bathroom

come over to your house

240 Can I _____ ? (너를 돕다)

241 Can I _____ ? (너와 함께 하다)

242 Can I _____ ? (너와 같이 가다)

243 Can I _____ ? (화장실에 가다)

244 Can I _____ now? (TV를 보다)

245 Can I _____ ? (너의 지우개를 빌리다)

246 Can I _____ ? (너의 집에 가다)

247 Can I _____ ? (내 친구를 집에 데려오다)

248 Can I _____ , please? (너의 주목을 받다)

Guess it!

⭐ In each picture, what would he or she most likely say?
Using '**Can I ~?**' make a sentence with the words or chunks below.

go with you	come over to your house	join you
have your attention	watch TV	bring my friend home
help you	borrow your eraser	go to the bathroom

1.

_____

_____ now?

2.

_____

_____ ?

3.

_____

_____ ?

Speak Up!

⭐ Complete the dialogues with the best sentence from this track.

> **보기**
>
> **A:** I will learn how to swim this vacation.
>
> **B:** I'm sorry. What did you say?
>
> **A:** **Can I have your attention**, please? I'm talking about my vacation plans!

1

A: Are you okay? 🎤 _____ ▶ ?

B: Yes, please. I have to carry this box outside.

A: No problem. Let's do it together.

Ⓡ

2

A: 🎤 _____ ▶ ? I think I lost mine.

B: You always lose things. Here you are.   *Here you are. 자, 여기 있어.

Ⓡ

3

A: Let's do homework together.

B: Sure. 🎤 _____ ▶ ?   *Sure. 그래.

A: I'm afraid not. How about your house?   *I'm afraid not. 안 될 것 같아.

Ⓡ

> 세이펜을 통해 각 상황에 맞는 말을 직접 녹음해 보고 확실히 익혔는지 확인해보세요.

📖 **[보기]** how to ~하는 방법 | vacation 방학   **1.** okay 괜찮은 | have to ~해야 한다 | outside 밖으로
2. lose[lost] 잃어버리다[잃어버렸다] | mine 나의 것   **3.** How about ~? ~은 어때?

Can you tell me why?

29 Track

너 ~할 수 있어? / 너 ~좀 해 줄래?

Say It! 1) 상대방이 뭔가를 할 수 있는지 물을 때
2) 상대방에게 부탁할 때

Fill it! Listen to the track and fill in the blanks with the correct sentence number.

Can you ~?

I.

H.

A.

B.

C.

G.

F.

E.

D.

249 Can you help me?

250 Can you swim well?

251 Can you play the piano?

252 Can you hold my bag?

253 Can you tell me why?

254 Can you save my seat?

255 Can you save one for me?

256 Can you solve the problem?

257 Can you explain that again?

Study words & chunks!

⭐ Choose the correct words or chunks for each sentence and fill in the blanks. ▷

swim well

save my seat

explain that again

tell me why

play the piano

help me

save one for me

hold my bag

solve the problem

249	Can you _____ ?	(나를 도와주다)
250	Can you _____ ?	(수영을 잘하다)
251	Can you _____ ?	(피아노를 치다)
252	Can you _____ ?	(내 가방을 들다)
253	Can you _____ ?	(나에게 이유를 말하다)
254	Can you _____ ?	(내 자리를 맡다)
255	Can you _____ ?	(나를 위해 한 개를 남겨두다)
256	Can you _____ ?	(그 문제를 해결하다)
257	Can you _____ ?	(그것을 다시 설명하다)

Guess it!

⭐ In each picture, what would he or she most likely say?
Using '**Can you ~?**' make a sentence with the words or chunks below.

hold my bag	save one for me	play the piano
solve the problem	save my seat	help me
explain that again	tell me why	swim well

1.
_____
_____ ?

2.
_____
_____ ?

3.
_____
_____ ?

Speak Up!

⭐ Complete the dialogues with the best sentence from this track.

> 보기
>
> **A: Can you play the piano?**
>
> B: Yes, but only a little. How about you?
>
> A: Me, too. I just started taking lessons.

1

A: 🎤 _____ ▷ ? I need to carry all these books.

B: Sure. Where should I put them?

*Sure. 물론이지.

Ⓡ

2

A: Come on, we need to go to music class.

B: I know, but I want to go to the bathroom first.

🎤 _____ ▷ ?

A: Okay. You can find me by the window.

Ⓡ

3

A: How do I get to the store?

B: Cross the street and go straight. Then turn right at ...

A: Wait! 🎤 _____ ▷ ? I missed it.

Ⓡ

세이펜을 통해 각 상황에 맞는 말을 직접 녹음해
보고 확실히 익혔는지 확인해보세요.

📖 **[보기]** How about ~? ~은 어때? | take lessons 수업을 받다 **1.** need to ~해야 한다 **2.** want to ~하고 싶다
| first 먼저 | by the window 창가에 **3.** How do I get to ~? ~에 어떻게 가야 돼? | go straight 똑바로 가다,
직진하다 | then 그다음에, 그러고 나서 | turn right 오른쪽으로 돌다 | miss[missed] 놓치다[놓쳤다]

I should get some sleep.

30
Track

나[너]는 ~해야 해. / 나는 ~해야겠어.

Say It! 내가 또는 상대방이 해야 하는 일을 말할 때
*should는 '~하는 게 좋겠어'와 같이 조언이나 충고를 표현할 수 있어요.

Fill it! Listen to the track and fill in the blanks with the correct sentence number.

I.

A.

B.

H.

I[You] should ~.

C.

G.

F.

E.

D.

258 I should stay home.

259 You should be on time.

260 I should get some sleep.

261 You should think about it.

262 I should try it again.

263 You should ask someone else.

264 You should keep your promise.

265 I should take the medicine.

266 You should stop complaining.

Study words & chunks!

⭐ Choose the correct words or chunks for each sentence and fill in the blanks. ▷

keep your promise

get some sleep

be on time

stay home

stop complaining

think about it

try it again

ask someone else

take the medicine

258 I should _____. (집에 머물다)

259 You should _____. (시간을 잘 지키다)

260 I should _____. (잠을 좀 자다)

261 You should _____. (그것에 대해 생각하다)

262 I should _____. (그것을 다시 해 보다)

263 You should _____. (다른 사람에게 물어보다)

264 You should _____. (너의 약속을 지키다)

265 I should _____. (약을 먹다)

266 You should _____. (그만 불평하다)

Guess it!

In each picture, what would he or she most likely say?
Using 'I[You] should ~.' make a sentence with the words or chunks below.

get some sleep	stay home	try it again
be on time	take the medicine	keep your promise
think about it	ask someone else	stop complaining

1.

2.

3.

Speak Up!

⭐ Complete the dialogues with the best sentence from this track.

> **보기**
>
> **A:** I can't solve this puzzle. It's too difficult.
>
> **B:** There is a hint on the next page.
>
> **A:** Really? **I should try it again**.

1

A: What are you going to do after school?

B: 🎤 _____ ▷. My grandmother will visit my family today.

Ⓡ

2

A: What's your topic for the speaking contest?

B: Umm... I don't know yet.

A: 🎤 _____ ▷. The contest is just next week!

Ⓡ

3

A: The movie starts at 3 p.m. tomorrow.

🎤 _____ ▷.

B: Okay. I won't be late this time.

A: Let's meet at 2:30, just to be sure.

Ⓡ

> 세이펜을 통해 각 상황에 맞는 말을 직접 녹음해 보고 확실히 익혔는지 확인해보세요.

📖 **[보기]** solve (문제를) 풀다 | hint 힌트 **1.** are[am, is] going to ~할 것이다 | grandmother 할머니 **2.** topic 주제 | speaking 말하기 | yet 아직 **3.** won't[will not] ~하지 않을 것이다 | this time 이번 | let's ~하자 | just to be sure 혹시나 해서

31 Track

You must be careful.

너는 반드시 ~해야 해.

Say It! 상대방이 꼭 해야 하는 일을 강하게 말할 때

Fill it! Listen to the track and fill in the blanks with the correct sentence number.

You must ~.

I.   A.   B.   C.   H.   G.   F.   E.   D.

267 You must be careful.
268 You must calm down.
269 You must choose only one.
270 You must listen to me first.
271 You must stop at the red light.
272 You must take care of your sister.
273 You must be here by nine o'clock.
274 You must be quiet during the movie.
275 You must wear a seatbelt every time.

Study words & chunks!

⭐ Choose the correct words or chunks for each sentence and fill in the blanks. ▷

be here

wear a seatbelt

take care of your sister

listen to me

be careful

be quiet

calm down

choose only one

stop at the red light

267 You must _____. (조심하다)

268 You must _____. (진정하다)

269 You must _____. (한 개만 고르다)

270 You must _____ first. (내 말을 듣다)

271 You must _____. (빨간불에 멈추다)

272 You must _____. (너의 여동생을 돌보다)

273 You must _____ by nine o'clock. (여기에 있다) * by ~까지는

274 You must _____ during the movie. (조용히 하다)

275 You must _____ every time. (안전벨트를 매다)

Guess it!

⭐ In each picture, what would he or she most likely say?
Using '**You must ~.**' make a sentence with the words or chunks below.

listen to me	wear a seatbelt	choose only one
calm down	take care of your sister	be quiet
stop at the red light	be here	be careful

1.

2.

3.

_____ every time.

Speak Up!

⭐ Complete the dialogues with the best sentence from this track.

> **보기**
>
> **A:** I didn't bring your books today. But I'll bring...
>
> **B:** What? I can't believe this! I told you...
>
> **A:** Hey! **You must listen to me** first. I can explain.

1

A: Why are you so angry? 🎤 _____ ▷.

B: But Jake keeps making fun of me.

A: Don't mind him. Then he will stop it.

Ⓡ

2

A: Hey, can I have some popcorn?

B: Shh... 🎤 _____ ▷ during the movie.

A: Just pass me some popcorn. Then, I will stop talking.

Ⓡ

3

A: Those are my favorite snacks! I want to buy them all.

B: 🎤 _____ ▷. We don't have enough money.

A: OK, then I will just get this one.

Ⓡ

세이펜을 통해 각 상황에 맞는 맞을 직접 녹음해
보고 확실히 익혔는지 확인해보세요.

📖 **[보기]** tell[told] 말하다[말했다] | explain 설명하다 **1.** so 그렇게 | Jake 제이크(남자 이름) | keep -ing 계속
~하다 | make fun of ~을 놀리다 | mind 신경 쓰다 | then 그러면 **2.** popcorn 팝콘 | pass 건네주다
3. snack 간식 | want to ~하고 싶다 | get 사다

32 Track

You might be right.

나[너]는 ~일지도 몰라(~일 수도 있어).

Say It! 확실하지 않은 생각이나 일어날 수도 있는 일에 대해 말할 때

Fill it! Listen to the track and fill in the blanks with the correct sentence number.

A.

B.

I.

I[You] might ~.

H.

C.

G.

F.

E.

D.

276 I might be in trouble.

277 I might change my mind.

278 I might be able to help.

279 You might be right.

280 You might be wrong.

281 You might be surprised.

282 You might get lucky.

283 You might get hurt.

284 You might have to wait a while.

Study words & chunks!

⭐ Choose the correct words or chunks for each sentence and fill in the blanks. ▶

be surprised

have to wait a while

be in trouble

be right

change my mind

be able to help

get hurt

be wrong

get lucky

276 I might _____ . (어려움에 처하다)

277 I might _____ . (내 생각을 바꾸다)

278 I might _____ . (도와줄 수 있다)

279 You might _____ . (옳다, 맞다)

280 You might _____ . (틀리다)

281 You might _____ . (놀라다)

282 You might _____ . (운이 좋다)

283 You might _____ . (다치다)

284 You might _____ . (잠깐 기다려야 한다)

Guess it!

⭐ In each picture, what would he or she most likely say?
Using 'I[You] might ~.' make a sentence with the words or chunks below.

have to wait a while	get hurt	be right
be wrong	be able to help	be in trouble
be surprised	get lucky	change my mind

1.
_____
_____ .

2.
_____
_____ .

3.
_____
_____ .

Speak Up!

⭐ Complete the dialogues with the best sentence from this track.

> **보기**
>
> **A:** I got 14 for this question. What about you?
>
> **B:** I got 11, but **you might be right**. I forgot to add at the end.

1

A: Where is Mom? I have to talk to her.

B: 🎤 _____ ▷. She went to get a perm.

A: When did she leave?

Ⓡ

2

A: Are you going to go with us for sure?

B: Umm... 🎤 _____ ▷. I want to stay home.

A: No way! I already bought your ticket!   *No way! 절대 안 돼!

Ⓡ

3

A: The pot is very hot. Be careful.

B: Don't worry. I will be fine.

A: You should use gloves. 🎤 _____ ▷.

Ⓡ

세이펜을 통해 각 상황에 맞는 말을 직접 녹음해 보고 확실히 익혔는지 확인해보세요.

📖 **[보기]** get[got] 얻다[얻었다] ｜ What about ~? ~은 어때? ｜ forget[forgot] to ~하는 것을 잊어버리다[잊어버렸다] **1.** have to ~해야 한다 ｜ go[went] 가다[갔다] ｜ get a perm 파마하다 ｜ leave 떠나다, 출발하다 **2.** for sure 확실히 ｜ buy[bought] 사다[샀다] ｜ ticket 입장권 **3.** pot 냄비

33 Track

I have to wash my hands.

나는 ~해야 해.

Say It! 내가 해야 하는 일을 말할 때
*have to는 should보다 해야 한다는 의미를 더 강하게 나타내요.

Fill it! Listen to the track and fill in the blanks with the correct sentence number.

I have to ~.

I.
A.
B.
H.
C.
G.
F.
E.
D.

285 I have to go out now.

286 I have to wash my hands.

287 I have to get a haircut.

288 I have to feed my dog.

289 I have to study for the test.

290 I have to make a choice.

291 I have to stop eating sweets.

292 I have to return this book tomorrow.

293 I have to change into my gym clothes.

Study words & chunks!

⭐ Choose the correct words or chunks for each sentence and fill in the blanks. ▷

return this book

stop eating sweets

study for the test

wash my hands

make a choice

feed my dog

go out

get a haircut

change into my gym clothes

285 I have to _____ now.   (나가다, 외출하다)

286 I have to _____.   (내 손을 씻다)

287 I have to _____.   (머리를 자르다)

288 I have to _____.   (나의 개에게 먹이를 주다)

289 I have to _____.   (시험공부를 하다)

290 I have to _____.   (선택하다)

291 I have to _____.   (단것들을 그만 먹다)

292 I have to _____ tomorrow.   (이 책을 반납하다)

293 I have to _____.   (내 체육복으로 갈아입다)

Guess it!

In each picture, what would he or she most likely say?
Using '**I have to ~.**' make a sentence with the words or chunks below.

feed my dog	go out	stop eating sweets
make a choice	change into my gym clothes	get a haircut
wash my hands	return this book	study for the test

1.
_____
_____ .

2.
_____
_____ .

3.
_____
_____ .

Speak Up!

⭐ Complete the dialogues with the best sentence from this track.

A: Come here and eat some pizza.

B: Wait a second. **I have to wash my hands**. I just got home.

1

A: What will you do tomorrow?

B: I will go to the library. 🎤 _____ ▷ tomorrow.

A: Did you finish reading that book? How was it?

ⓡ

2

A: Why don't we watch a movie after school?

B: What? We have an exam tomorrow! 🎤 _____

_____ ▷ .

A: Ah! I completely forgot about it.

ⓡ

3

A: There are two birthday parties on Saturday. Both start at twelve.

B: That's too bad. You can't go to both.   *That's too bad. 그것 참 안됐다.

A: I know. 🎤 _____ ▷ .

ⓡ

> 세이펜을 통해 각 상황에 맞는 말을 직접 녹음해
> 보고 확실히 익혔는지 확인해보세요.

📑 **[보기]** second (아주) 잠깐 | get[got] home 집에 도착하다[도착했다] **2.** Why don't we ~? 우리 ~하는 게 어때?
| completely 완전히 | forget[forgot] about ~에 대해 잊어버리다[잊어버렸다] **3.** Saturday 토요일

34
Track

You have to see this!

너는 ~해야 해.

Say It! 상대방이 해야 하는 일을 말할 때
*have to는 should보다 해야 한다는 의미를 더 강하게 나타내요.

Fill it! Listen to the track and fill in the blanks with the correct sentence number.

I.

A.

B.

C.

H.

You have to ~.

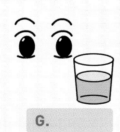

G.

F.

E.

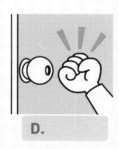

D.

294 You have to go now.

295 You have to see this!

296 You have to believe me.

297 You have to decide now.

298 You have to stand in line.

299 You have to make sure.

300 You have to let it go.

301 You have to come back by six.

302 You have to knock on the door.

Study words & chunks!

⭐ Choose the correct words or chunks for each sentence and fill in the blanks. ▷

see this

come back

stand in line

knock on the door

go

let it go

make sure

decide

believe me

294 You have to _____ now. (가다)

295 You have to _____ ! (이것을 보다)

296 You have to _____ . (나를 믿다)

297 You have to _____ now. (결정하다)

298 You have to _____ . (한 줄로 서다)

299 You have to _____ . (확인하다)

300 You have to _____ . (잊어버리다, 내버려두다)

301 You have to _____ by six. (돌아오다)

302 You have to _____ . (문을 두드리다, 문을 노크하다)

Guess it!

In each picture, what would he or she most likely say?
Using '**You have to ~.**' make a sentence with the words or chunks below.

let it go	go	stand in line
see this	come back	believe me
decide	make sure	knock on the door

1.

_____

_____ !

2.

_____

_____ .

3.

_____

_____ .

Speak Up!

⭐ Complete the dialogues with the best sentence from this track.

> **A:** He spilled milk on your desk and didn't clean it.
>
> **B:** Are you sure?
>
> **A:** Yes! **You have to believe me**. I saw it!

1

A: I have to return this book today. What time does the library close?

B: It will close soon. 🎤 _____ ▷ now.

Ⓡ

2

A: Why are you still upset?

B: Jake keeps calling me by my nickname!

A: 🎤 _____ ▷. He calls everyone by their nickname.

Ⓡ

3

A: Which one do you want? 🎤 _____ ▷ now.

B: Now? But I need more time to think!

A: Okay. Then, I'll give you just ten seconds.

Ⓡ

세이펜을 통해 각 상황에 맞는 말을 직접 녹음해 보고 확실히 익혔는지 확인해보세요.

📖 **[보기]** spill[spilled] 쏟다[쏟았다] | sure 확실한 | see[saw] 보다[봤다] **1.** return 반납하다 | soon 곧 **2.** still 아직도 | upset 속상한 | Jake 제이크(남자 이름) | keep –ing 계속 ~하다 | nickname 별명 | everyone 모든 사람 **3.** which 어느, 어떤 | more 더 (많이) | second (시간) 초

35 Track

You don't have to worry.

너는 ~할 필요가 없어(~하지 않아도 돼).

Say It! 상대방이 하지 않아도 되는 일에 대해 말할 때

Fill it! Listen to the track and fill in the blanks with the correct sentence number.

You don't have to ~.

I.　A.　B.　C.　H.　G.　F.　E.　D.

303　You don't have to be sorry.
304　You don't have to get angry.
305　You don't have to worry.
306　You don't have to wait for me.
307　You don't have to decide now.
308　You don't have to tell me.
309　You don't have to answer me.
310　You don't have to thank me.
311　You don't have to do it right now.

Study words & chunks!

⭐ Choose the correct words or chunks for each sentence and fill in the blanks. ▷

decide

worry

do it

be sorry

answer me

thank me

wait for me

get angry

tell me

303	You don't have to _____ .	(미안해하다)
304	You don't have to _____ .	(화를 내다)
305	You don't have to _____ .	(걱정하다)
306	You don't have to _____ .	(나를 기다리다)
307	You don't have to _____ now.	(결정하다)
308	You don't have to _____ .	(나에게 말하다)
309	You don't have to _____ .	(나에게 대답하다)
310	You don't have to _____ .	(나에게 고마워하다)
311	You don't have to _____ right now.	(그것을 하다)

Guess it!

⭐ In each picture, what would he or she most likely say?
Using '**You don't have to ~.**' make a sentence with the words or chunks below.

do it	answer me	thank me
be sorry	worry	decide
wait for me	get angry	tell me

1.
_____
_____.

2.
_____
_____.

3.
_____
_____ right now.

Speak Up!

⭐ Complete the dialogues with the best sentence from this track.

> **보기**
>
> **A:** Do you want to go to the movies this weekend?
>
> **B:** I am not sure.
>
> **A:** **You don't have to decide** now. Just tell me before Friday.

1

A: Thank you. That was a big help.

B: 🎤 _____ ▷. It was her idea.

Ⓡ

2

A: Guess who she likes!

B: 🎤 _____ ▷. It's her secret.

A: You are right. I should keep her secret.

Ⓡ

3

A: 🎤 _____ ▷. You can go first.

B: I can wait for you. We are not in a hurry.

Ⓡ

세이펜을 통해 각 상황에 맞는 말을 직접 녹음해
보고 확실히 익혔는지 확인해보세요.

📖 **[보기]** want to ～하고 싶다 | sure 확실한 | Friday 금요일 **2.** keep a secret 비밀을 지키다 **3.** first 먼저 |
in a hurry 바쁜

36

Track

I had to stay after class.

나는 ~해야 했어.

Say It! 내가 과거에 해야 했던 일을 말할 때

Fill it! Listen to the track and fill in the blanks with the correct sentence number.

I had to ~.

I. ___ A. ___ B. ___ H. ___ C. ___ G. ___ F. ___ E. ___ D. ___

312 I had to go home early.

313 I had to think a little bit.

314 I had to stay after class.

315 I had to wait a long time.

316 I had to go there by myself.

317 I had to run an errand.

318 I had to clean up my own mess.

319 I had to explain everything.

320 I had to choose between the two.

Study words & chunks!

⭐ Choose the correct words or chunks for each sentence and fill in the blanks. ▷

go home early

run an errand

think a little bit

wait a long time

explain everything

choose between the two

stay after class

clean up my own mess

go there by myself

312 I had to _____ . (집에 일찍 가다)

313 I had to _____ . (조금 생각하다)

314 I had to _____ . (수업이 끝나고 남다)

315 I had to _____ . (오래 기다리다)

316 I had to _____ . (혼자 그곳에 가다)

317 I had to _____ . (심부름하다)

318 I had to _____ . (내가 어지럽힌 것을 치우다)

319 I had to _____ . (모든 것을 설명하다)

320 I had to _____ . (둘 중에서 고르다)

Guess it!

In each picture, what would he or she most likely say?
Using '**I had to ~.**' make a sentence with the words or chunks below.

think a little bit	wait a long time	go there by myself
stay after class	explain everything	run an errand
choose between the two	clean up my own mess	go home early

1. _____
   _____ .

2. _____
   _____ .

3. _____
   _____ .

Speak Up!

⭐ Complete the dialogues with the best sentence from this track.

> **A:** What took you so long? Were there a lot of people in line?
>
> **B:** Yes. **I had to wait a long time**.
>
> **A:** Let's eat. I'm starving.   *I'm starving. 배고파 죽겠어.

1

A: 🎤 _____ ▷.

B: Why? Did you do something wrong?

A: I didn't do my homework again. My teacher got mad at me.   Ⓡ

2

A: I'm so sorry about yesterday. 🎤 _____ ▷.

B: What happened?

A: My grandma was very sick, so I visited her in the hospital.   Ⓡ

3

A: Why are you late? We were waiting for you.

B: Sorry. 🎤 _____ ▷. My mom needed salt for cooking.   Ⓡ

세이펜을 통해 각 상황에 맞는 말을 직접 녹음해 보고 확실히 익혔는지 확인해보세요.

📖 **[보기]** take[took] long 시간이 오래 걸리다[걸렸다] | so 그렇게 | a lot of 많은 | let's ~하자　**1.** something 무엇 | get[got] mad at ~에게 화를 내다[냈다]　**2.** happen[happened] (일이) 일어나다[일어났다] | grandma 할머니 | so 그래서

37
Track

I used to hate carrots.

나는 ~했었어(~하곤 했어).

 Say It! 나의 과거의 상태나 내가 과거에 했던 행동에 대해 말할 때
*지금은 그렇지 않다는 의미까지 나타내요.

Fill it! Listen to the track and fill in the blanks with the correct sentence number.

I.

A.

B.

H.

I used to ~.

C.

G.

F.

E.

D.

321 I used to hate carrots.

322 I used to have a hamster.

323 I used to have curly hair.

324 I used to have a lot of toys.

325 I used to live near here.

326 I used to play with my friends here.

327 I used to go to the dentist often.

328 I used to go swimming once a week.

329 I used to enjoy playing with Lego blocks.

Study words & chunks!

⭐ Choose the correct words or chunks for each sentence and fill in the blanks. ▷

go swimming

hate carrots

have curly hair

have a lot of toys

go to the dentist

live near here

play with my friends

enjoy playing with Lego blocks

have a hamster

321 I used to _____ . (당근들을 싫어하다)

322 I used to _____ . (햄스터를 기르다)

323 I used to _____ . (곱슬머리이다)

324 I used to _____ . (장난감들이 많이 있다)

325 I used to _____ . (이 근처에 살다)

326 I used to _____ here. (내 친구들과 놀다)

327 I used to _____ often. (치과에 가다)

328 I used to _____ once a week. (수영하러 가다) * once a week 일주일에 한 번

329 I used to _____ . (레고 블록들을 가지고 노는 것을 즐기다)

Guess it!

⭐ In each picture, what would he or she most likely say?
Using 'I **used to** ~.' make a sentence with the words or chunks below.

enjoy playing with Lego blocks	go to the dentist	have curly hair
have a hamster	live near here	hate carrots
go swimming	have a lot of toys	play with my friends

1.

_____

_____ here.

2.

_____

_____

3.

_____

_____ .

Speak Up!

⭐ Complete the dialogues with the best sentence from this track.

> **보기**
>
> A: You don't have any toys in your room.
>
> B: **I used to have a lot of toys**. But I gave them to the kid next door.

1

A: You ate all the carrots in the curry. You must like them.

B: 🎤 _____ ▷. But I like them now.

A: Really? I still don't like them.

Ⓡ

2

A: 🎤 _____ ▷ often.

B: Why? Did you have bad teeth?

A: Yes, but my teeth are all fine now.

Ⓡ

3

A: 🎤 _____ ▷ once a week. But I can't these days.

B: Why did you stop?

A: I hurt my leg.

Ⓡ

세이펜을 통해 각 상황에 맞는 말을 직접 녹음해 보고 확실히 익혔는지 확인해보세요.

📖 **[보기]** give[gave] 주다[주었다] | next door 옆집에 사는 **1.** eat[ate] 먹다[먹었다] | curry 카레 | must ~임이 틀림없다 | really 정말 | still 아직도 **2.** bad teeth (여러 개의) 충치 **3.** these days 요즘에는 | hurt[hurt] 다치게 하다[다치게 했다]

38

Track

I was disappointed.

나는 ~했어.

Say It! 내가 과거에 어떤 상태였는지 말할 때

Fill it! Listen to the track and fill in the blanks with the correct sentence number.

I.

A.

B.

I was ~.

H.

C.

G.

F.

E.

D.

330 I was tired.

331 I was wrong.

332 I was surprised.

333 I was disappointed.

334 I was a little upset.

335 I was really worried.

336 I was happy and excited.

337 I was late for school.

338 I was sick with a cold.

Study words & chunks!

⭐ Choose the correct words or chunks for each sentence and fill in the blanks. ▷

happy and excited

disappointed

a little upset

sick with a cold

surprised

tired

late for school

wrong

really worried

330 I was _____. (피곤한)

331 I was _____. (틀린)

332 I was _____. (놀란)

333 I was _____. (실망한)

334 I was _____. (조금 속상한)

335 I was _____. (매우 걱정하는)

336 I was _____. (행복하고 신이 나는)

337 I was _____. (학교에 지각한)

338 I was _____. (감기에 걸려 아픈)

Guess it!

⭐ In each picture, what would he or she most likely say?
   Using '**I was ~.**' make a sentence with the words or chunks below.

really worried	tired	surprised
wrong	happy and excited	late for school
a little upset	sick with a cold	disappointed

1. _____

2. _____

3. _____

Speak Up!

⭐ Complete the dialogues with the best sentence from this track.

> 보기
>
> **A:** Where are your glasses?
>
> **B:** My brother broke my glasses by mistake. **I was a little upset**.
>
> **A:** I am sure you were.

1

A: Why were you absent from school yesterday?

B: 🎤 _____ ▷ .

A: Oh, did you see the doctor?

B: Yes, I did. I am fine now.

Ⓡ

2

A: I fell asleep early yesterday. 🎤 _____ ▷ .

B: I see. What did you do?

*I see. 그렇구나.

A: I played soccer all day with my friends.

Ⓡ

3

A: You scored 100 on the math test! Good job!　　*Good job! 잘했어!

B: Thanks! 🎤 _____ ▷ . I wasn't expecting much.

Ⓡ

> 세이펜을 통해 각 상황에 맞는 말을 직접 녹음해 보고 확실히 익혔는지 확인해보세요.

📖 **[보기]** glasses 안경 ｜ break[broke] 부러뜨리다[부러뜨렸다] ｜ by mistake 실수로 ｜ sure 확실한　**1.** absent from ~에 결석한 ｜ see a doctor 병원에 가다　**2.** fall[fell] asleep 잠들다[잠들었다] ｜ all day 하루 종일　**3.** score[scored] 점수를 받다[받았다] ｜ expect 기대하다

39 Track

He was very busy.

그[그녀]는 ~했어.

Say It! 다른 사람이 과거에 어떤 상태였는지 말할 때

Fill it! Listen to the track and fill in the blanks with the correct sentence number.

I.

A.

B.

Welcome to your New class!
H.

He[She] was ~.

C.

G.

F.

E.

D.

---

339 She was funny.

340 He was still asleep.

341 He was very busy.

342 He was very friendly.

343 She was very helpful.

344 He was so shy.

345 She was so nice to me.

346 She was angry with me.

347 He was sure about that.

Study words & chunks!

⭐ Choose the correct words or chunks for each sentence and fill in the blanks. ▷

so nice to me

angry with me

very helpful

funny

sure about that

still asleep

very busy

so shy

very friendly

339	She was _____.	(재미있는, 웃기는)
340	He was _____.	(아직 자고 있는)
341	He was _____.	(매우 바쁜)
342	He was _____.	(매우 친절한)
343	She was _____.	(정말 도움이 되는)
344	He was _____.	(매우 수줍어하는)
345	She was _____.	(나에게 매우 다정한)
346	She was _____.	(나에게 화가 난)
347	He was _____.	(그것에 대해 확신하는)

Guess it!

⭐ In each picture, what would he or she most likely say?
Using '**He[She] was ~.**' make a sentence with the words or chunks below.

so nice to me	angry with me	sure about that
funny	so shy	still asleep
very friendly	very busy	very helpful

1.
_____
_____.

2.
_____
_____.

3.
_____
_____.

Speak Up!

⭐ Complete the dialogues with the best sentence from this track.

> **A:** Did you tell Bill about our plan?
>
> **B:** Not yet. **He was very busy**.
>
> **A:** Okay, but tell him soon.

1

A: Wow. Did he really say that?

B: Yes. 🎤 _____ ▷.

A: But I don't believe him. He always lies.

Ⓡ

2

A: You look so upset. What's wrong?

B: I put on my sister's dress without telling her.

🎤 _____ ▷.

Ⓡ

3

A: I visited my grandmother yesterday.

B: Did you have fun?

A: Yes. 🎤 _____ ▷. She bought me new shoes.

Ⓡ

세이펜을 통해 각 상황에 맞는 말을 직접 녹음해 보고 확실히 익혔는지 확인해보세요.

📖 **[보기]** Bill 빌(남자 이름) | yet 아직 | soon 빨리; 곧 **2.** upset 속상한 | put[put] on ~을 입다[입었다] | dress 원피스, 드레스 | without -ing ~하지 않고 **3.** grandmother 할머니 | have fun 재미있게 놀다 | buy[bought] 사 주다[사 줬다]

40 Track

I went to the bathroom.

나는 ~에 갔어.

Say It! 내가 과거에 어디에 갔는지 말할 때

Fill it! Listen to the track and fill in the blanks with the correct sentence number.

I.

A.

B.

C.

H.

I went to ~.

G.

F.

E.

D.

348 I went to bed.

349 I went to the bathroom.

350 I went to the science museum.

351 I went to the playground.

352 I went to the supermarket.

353 I went to the movie theater.

354 I went to a baseball game.

355 I went to a swimming pool.

356 I went to my friend's birthday party.

Study words & chunks!

⭐ Choose the correct words or chunks for each sentence and fill in the blanks. ▷

bed

the playground

the science museum

the bathroom

my friend's birthday party

the movie theater

a swimming pool

the supermarket

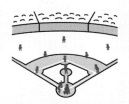

a baseball game

348 I went to _____. (침대)

349 I went to _____. (화장실)

350 I went to _____. (과학박물관)

351 I went to _____. (놀이터)

352 I went to _____. (슈퍼마켓)

353 I went to _____. (영화관)

354 I went to _____. (야구 경기)

355 I went to _____. (수영장)

356 I went to _____. (내 친구의 생일 파티)

Guess it!

★ In each picture, what would he or she most likely say?
Using '**I went to ~.**' make a sentence with the words or chunks below.

my friend's birthday party	a baseball game	the playground
the bathroom	the science museum	the movie theater
the supermarket	a swimming pool	bed

1.

_____

2.

_____

3.

_____

Speak Up!

⭐ Complete the dialogues with the best sentence from this track.

> **보기**
>
> A: **I went to the playground**.
>
> B: What did you do there?
>
> A: I played on the swings with my sister. It was fun.

1

A: What did you do last weekend?

B: 🎤 _____ ▷. My favorite team

won the game!

A: Awesome!

Ⓡ

2

A: 🎤 _____ ▷.

B: Really? What was the best part?

A: The robots were my favorite.

Ⓡ

3

A: Did you do anything special yesterday?

B: 🎤 _____ ▷. I had fun in the water.

A: That sounds great!

Ⓡ

세이펜을 통해 각 상황에 맞는 말을 직접 녹음해
보고 확실히 익혔는지 확인해보세요.

📖 **[보기]** play[played] on the swings 그네를 타다[탔다]   **1.** win[won] 이기다[이겼다] | awesome 굉장한, 아주
멋진   **2.** best 최고의, 제일 좋은 | robot 로봇   **3.** special 특별한 | have[had] fun 재미있게 놀다[놀았다]

I put it on the desk.

나는 그것을 ~에 두었어(놓았어).

Say It! 내가 물건을 어디에 두었는지 말할 때

Fill it! Listen to the track and fill in the blanks with the correct sentence number.

I.

A.

B.

I put it ~.

C.

H.

G.

F.

E.

D.

357 I put it in the box.

358 I put it in my pocket.

359 I put it in my backpack.

360 I put it in the drawer.

361 I put it in the fridge.

362 I put it on the floor.

363 I put it on the table.

364 I put it on the desk.

365 I put it under my bed.

Study words & chunks!

⭐ Choose the correct words or chunks for each sentence and fill in the blanks. ▶

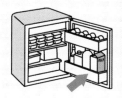

in the fridge

on the desk

in the box

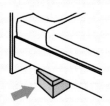

under my bed

in my backpack

on the table

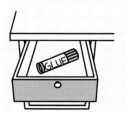

in the drawer

on the floor

in my pocket

357	I put it _____ .	(상자 안에)
358	I put it _____ .	(내 주머니 안에)
359	I put it _____ .	(내 책가방 안에)
360	I put it _____ .	(서랍 안에)
361	I put it _____ .	(냉장고 안에)
362	I put it _____ .	(바닥 위에)
363	I put it _____ .	(테이블 위에)
364	I put it _____ .	(책상 위에)
365	I put it _____ .	(내 침대 밑에)

Guess it!

⭐ In each picture, what would he or she most likely say?
Using 'I put it ~.' make a sentence with the words or chunks below.

in my pocket	on the floor	on the desk
under my bed	in the box	in my backpack
in the drawer	on the table	in the fridge

1.
_____
_____ .

2.
_____
_____ .

3.
_____
_____ .

Speak Up!

⭐ Complete the dialogues with the best sentence from this track.

> **보기**
>
> **A:** Where is the water bottle?
>
> **B: I put it in the fridge**.
>
> **A:** Oh, thanks. I wanted cold water.

1

A: Do we have a flashlight? It's too dark under the bed.

B: What are you looking for?

A: I am looking for my old toy box. 🎤 _____ ▷. Ⓡ

2

A: I am looking for my blue cap. Where did you put it?

B: Check your closet. 🎤 _____ ▷. Ⓡ

3

A: Oh, no! I think I lost my wallet. I can't find it in my backpack.

B: Maybe you left it at home.

A: No. 🎤 _____ ▷. Where did it go? Ⓡ

> 세이펜을 통해 각 상황에 맞는 말을 직접 녹음해 보고 확실히 익혔는지 확인해보세요.

📖 **1.** flashlight 손전등 | too 너무 | look for ~을 찾다 **2.** closet 옷장 **3.** lose[lost] 잃어버리다[잃어버렸다] | wallet 지갑 | maybe 아마 | leave[left] 두고 오다[두고 왔다]

42 Track

I didn't eat dinner.

나는 ～하지 않았어.

Say It! 내가 과거에 하지 않은 일을 말할 때
*didn't는 did not을 줄인 말이에요.

Fill it! Listen to the track and fill in the blanks with the correct sentence number.

I.

A.

B.

C.

H.

I didn't ~.

G.

F.

E.

D.

366 I didn't say that.

367 I didn't eat dinner.

368 I didn't lie to you.

369 I didn't sleep enough.

370 I didn't bring an umbrella.

371 I didn't tell anyone.

372 I didn't hear anything.

373 I didn't mean that.

374 I didn't do anything wrong.

Study words & chunks!

⭐ Choose the correct words or chunks for each sentence and fill in the blanks. ▷

say that

tell anyone

lie to you

do anything wrong

hear anything

eat dinner

sleep enough

bring an umbrella

mean that

366 I didn't _____. (그것을 말하다)

367 I didn't _____. (저녁을 먹다)

368 I didn't _____. (너에게 거짓말하다)

369 I didn't _____. (충분히 자다)

370 I didn't _____. (우산을 가져오다)

371 I didn't _____. (누군가에게 말하다)

372 I didn't _____. (무언가를 듣다)

373 I didn't _____. (그것을 의미하다)

374 I didn't _____. (무언가 잘못된 것을 하다)

Guess it!

⭐ In each picture, what would he or she most likely say?
Using 'I didn't ~.' make a sentence with the words or chunks below.

tell anyone	mean that	lie to you
sleep enough	say that	bring an umbrella
do anything wrong	eat dinner	hear anything

1. _____

_____ .

2. _____

_____ .

3. _____

_____ .

Speak Up!

⭐ Complete the dialogues with the best sentence from this track.

> **보기**
>
> **A:** I told my secret only to you. But everyone knows it now.
>
> **B:** It wasn't me! **I didn't tell anyone**.

1

A: Where is your hat?

B: I took it off. You said it looked funny.

A: 🎤 _____ ▷. I was kidding.

Ⓡ

2

A: Our teacher is calling you. Go to the teachers' room now.

B: Why? 🎤 _____ ▷.

A: I don't know. Maybe it's nothing.

Ⓡ

3

A: I heard some strange sounds outside. Did you hear that?

B: No, 🎤 _____ ▷.

A: I did. I think something is out there.

Ⓡ

> 세이펜을 통해 각 상황에 맞는 말을 직접 녹음해
> 보고 확실히 익혔는지 확인해보세요.

📖 **[보기]** tell[told] 말하다[말했다] | secret 비밀 | everyone 모든 사람 **1.** take[took] off (옷, 모자 등을) 벗다
[벗었다] | say[said] 말하다[말했다] | look[looked] ~해 보이다[보였다] | funny 우스운 | kid 농담하다
2. teachers' room 교무실 | maybe 아마도 **3.** hear[heard] 듣다[들었다] | strange 이상한 | outside 밖에서

Did you get hurt?

Track 43

너는 ~했어?

Say It! 상대방에게 어떤 행동을 했는지 물어볼 때

Fill it! Listen to the track and fill in the blanks with the correct sentence number.

I.

A.

B.

H.

Did you ~?

C.

G.

F.

E.

D.

375 Did you get hurt?

376 Did you bring my book?

377 Did you finish your homework?

378 Did you see the TV show?

379 Did you hear the news?

380 Did you get my message?

381 Did you get a good grade?

382 Did you go anywhere interesting?

383 Did you have fun on your birthday?

Study words & chunks!

⭐ Choose the correct words or chunks for each sentence and fill in the blanks. ▷

go anywhere interesting

get a good grade

bring my book

have fun on your birthday

hear the news

get hurt

get my message

see the TV show

finish your homework

375	Did you _____ ? (다치다)
376	Did you _____ ? (내 책을 가져오다)
377	Did you _____ ? (너의 숙제를 끝내다)
378	Did you _____ ? (그 TV 쇼를 보다)
379	Did you _____ ? (그 소식을 듣다)
380	Did you _____ ? (내 메시지를 받다)
381	Did you _____ ? (좋은 성적을 받다)
382	Did you _____ ? (재미있는 어딘가에 가다)
383	Did you _____ ? (너의 생일에 재미있게 놀다)

Guess it!

⭐ In each picture, what would he or she most likely say?
Using '**Did you ~?**' make a sentence with the words or chunks below.

hear the news	get a good grade	get my message
have fun on your birthday	get hurt	go anywhere interesting
finish your homework	bring my book	see the TV show

1.

_____

_____ ?

2.

_____

_____ ?

3.

_____

_____ ?

Speak Up!

⭐ Complete the dialogues with the best sentence from this track.

> 보기
>
> **A: Did you bring my book**? I lent it to you last week.
>
> B: Oh, no! I forgot. I'm so sorry.
>
> A: It's okay. You can give it back tomorrow.

1

A: 🎙 _____ ▷ ? I asked you something.

B: No, I didn't check. What was it about?

A: It was about our vacation day.

Ⓡ

2

A: 🎙 _____ ▷ ? We have no class this Friday!

B: I didn't know that. That is great!

A: We are free on that day. Hurray!

*Hurray! 만세!

Ⓡ

3

A: I had a lot of fun yesterday.

B: 🎙 _____ ▷ ?

A: Yes. I went to an amusement park with my family.

Ⓡ

> 세이펜을 통해 각 상황에 맞는 말을 직접 녹음해
> 보고 확실히 익혔는지 확인해보세요.

📖📖 **[보기]** lend[lent] 빌려주다[빌려주었다] | forget[forgot] 잊다[잊었다] **1.** something 무엇 **2.** Friday 금요일
3. have[had] a lot of fun 아주 재미있게 놀다[놀았다] | go[went] 가다[갔다] | amusement park 놀이공원

정답과 해설 p.15

44 Track

We will wait for you.

나[우리]는 ~할 거야(할게).

Say It! 내가 또는 우리가 앞으로 할 일에 대해 말할 때
*I[We] will을 줄여서 I'll, We'll이라고 쓰기도 해요.

Fill it! Listen to the track and fill in the blanks with the correct sentence number.

I.

A.

B.

H.

I[We] will ~.

C.

G.

F.

E.

D.

384 I will be there soon.

385 We will wait for you.

386 I will take this one.

387 I will call you later.

388 I will tell you everything.

389 We will go on a trip.

390 I will give it a try.

391 I will explain it later.

392 I will wake up early tomorrow.

Study words & chunks!

⭐ Choose the correct words or chunks for each sentence and fill in the blanks. ▶

give it a try

wait for you

call you

explain it

go on a trip

wake up early

tell you everything

be there

take this one

384 I will _____ soon. (그곳에 있다) * soon 곧

385 We will _____ . (너를 기다리다)

386 I will _____ . (이것을 고르다, 이것을 사다)

387 I will _____ later. (너에게 전화하다) * later 나중에

388 I will _____ . (너에게 모든 것을 말하다)

389 We will _____ . (여행을 가다)

390 I will _____ . (한번 해 보다)

391 I will _____ later. (그것을 설명하다)

392 I will _____ tomorrow. (일찍 일어나다)

Guess it!

⭐ In each picture, what would he or she most likely say?
Using 'I[We] will ~.' make a sentence with the words or chunks below.

call you	go on a trip	wait for you
wake up early	be there	tell you everything
take this one	give it a try	explain it

1.

_____
_____.

2.

_____
_____.

3.

_____
_____.

Speak Up!

⭐ Complete the dialogues with the best sentence from this track.

> **보기**
>
> **A:** What happened to your arm?
>
> **B:** It's a long story. **I will explain it** later.
>
> **A:** Okay. Let's go to class.

1

A: I left my cap at school.

B: Don't worry. 🎤 _____ ▷.

A: Thanks. I will be back soon.

Ⓡ

2

A: I want to ask you something. Are you busy now?

B: Sorry. I have to go home now. 🎤 _____ ▷ later.

A: Okay. Then, call me after five o'clock.

Ⓡ

3

A: 🎤 _____ ▷ tomorrow.

B: I don't believe you. You always sleep in.

A: I am serious this time.

Ⓡ

세이펜을 통해 각 상황에 맞는 말을 직접 녹음해 보고 확실히 익혔는지 확인해보세요.

📖 **[보기]** happen[happened] (일이) 일어나다[일어났다] | let's ～하자 **1.** leave[left] 두고 오다[두고 왔다] | be back 돌아오다 **2.** want to ～하고 싶다 | then 그러면 **3.** sleep in 늦잠을 자다 | serious 진심인, 진지한 | this time 이번

정답과 해설 p.16

She will be all right.

45

그[그녀]는 ~할 거야.

Say It! 다른 사람이 앞으로 무엇을 할지, 어떤 상태일지 말할 때
*He[She] will을 줄여서 He'll, She'll이라고 쓰기도 해요.

Fill it! Listen to the track and fill in the blanks with the correct sentence number.

I.

A.

B.

H.

He[She] will ~.

C.

G.

F.

E.

D.

393 He will be late.

394 She will be all right.

395 She will be very upset.

396 He will come later.

397 He will join our team.

398 She will understand you.

399 He will bring it back tomorrow.

400 She will wait for us.

401 He will buy me ice cream.

Study words & chunks!

⭐ Choose the correct words or chunks for each sentence and fill in the blanks. ▷

join our team

be all right

wait for us

be very upset

bring it back

understand you

come later

buy me ice cream

be late

393 He will _____ . (늦다, 지각하다)

394 She will _____ . (괜찮다)

395 She will _____ . (매우 속상하다)

396 He will _____ . (나중에 오다)

397 He will _____ . (우리 팀에 함께하다)

398 She will _____ . (너를 이해하다)

399 He will _____ tomorrow. (그것을 되돌려주다)

400 She will _____ . (우리를 기다리다)

401 He will _____ . (나에게 아이스크림을 사주다)

Guess it!

⭐ In each picture, what would he or she most likely say?
Using '**He[She] will ~.**' make a sentence with the words or chunks below.

join our team	bring it back	be all right
be very upset	be late	wait for us
buy me ice cream	come later	understand you

1.
_____
_____.

2.
_____
_____.

3.
_____
_____.

Speak Up!

⭐ Complete the dialogues with the best sentence from this track.

> A: We are late. She is there already!
>
> B: It's okay. **She will wait for us**.
>
> A: Don't you feel sorry for her? Let's hurry up.

1

A: She is angry with me. What should I do?

B: Say sorry to her. 🎤 _____ ▷. Ⓡ

2

A: Did you lend your book to him?

B: Yes. 🎤 _____ ▷ tomorrow. Why? Ⓡ

A: I want to borrow it, too.

3

A: Kate is absent from school today.

B: Is she still sick? I'm worried.

A: I heard she's getting better. 🎤 _____ ▷. Ⓡ

세이펜을 통해 각 상황에 맞는 말을 직접 녹음해 보고 확실히 익혔는지 확인해보세요.

📖 [보기] Don't you ~? 너는 ～하지 않니? **2.** lend 빌려주다 ｜ want to ～하고 싶다 **3.** Kate 케이트(여자 이름) ｜ absent from ～에 결석한 ｜ still 아직도 ｜ worried 걱정하는 ｜ hear[heard] 듣다[들었다] ｜ get better 나아지다, 좋아지다

I won't tell anybody.

46 Track

나는 ~하지 않을 거야(~않을게).

Say It! 내가 앞으로 하지 않을 일에 대해 말할 때
*won't는 will not을 줄인 말이에요.

Fill it! Listen to the track and fill in the blanks with the correct sentence number.

I won't ~.

I.

A.

B.

C.

H.

G.

F.

E.

D.

402 I won't be there.

403 I won't be late again.

404 I won't do it again.

405 I won't tell anybody.

406 I won't lie to you.

407 I won't give up.

408 I won't get mad.

409 I won't bother you.

410 I won't make a mistake.

Study words & chunks!

⭐ Choose the correct words or chunks for each sentence and fill in the blanks. ▶

tell anybody

give up

get mad

bother you

make a mistake

lie to you

be there

do it

be late

402 I won't _____. (그곳에 있다)

403 I won't _____ again. (늦다, 지각하다)

404 I won't _____ again. (그것을 하다)

405 I won't _____. (누군가에게 말하다)

406 I won't _____. (너에게 거짓말하다)

407 I won't _____. (포기하다)

408 I won't _____. (화를 내다)

409 I won't _____. (너를 귀찮게 하다)

410 I won't _____. (실수를 하다)

Guess it!

⭐ In each picture, what would he or she most likely say?
Using '**I won't ~.**' make a sentence with the words or chunks below.

lie to you	do it	tell anybody
get mad	be late	make a mistake
be there	give up	bother you

1. _____ again.

2. _____

3. _____

Speak Up!

⭐ Complete the dialogues with the best sentence from this track.

> **보기**
>
> A: Will I see you at the birthday party?
>
> B: I am sorry. **I won't be there**. I have to visit my grandfather.

1

A: Who spilled water on my book?

B: I don't know. I didn't see anybody.

A: Just tell me who. 🎤 _____ ▷ . ⓡ

2

A: Why are you crying?

B: Leave me alone. I don't want to talk about it.   *Leave me alone. 나 좀 내버려 둬.

A: Sorry. 🎤 _____ ▷ . ⓡ

3

A: I want to play soccer, too. Can I join your team?

B: You have to play well. This match is very important.

A: Don't worry. 🎤 _____ ▷ . ⓡ

세이펜을 통해 각 상황에 맞는 말을 직접 녹음해 보고 확실히 익혔는지 확인해보세요.

📖 **[보기]** have to ～해야 한다   **1.** spill[spilled] 쏟다[쏟았다]   **2.** leave ～한 상태로 두다, 내버려 두다   **3.** match 경기, 시합

47 Track

I'll be able to join you.

나는 ~할 수 있을 거야.

Say It! 내가 앞으로 할 수 있는 일에 대해 말할 때
*I'll은 I will을 줄인 말이에요.

Fill it! Listen to the track and fill in the blanks with the correct sentence number.

I'll be able to ~.

I. 　　　　A. 　　　　B. 　　　　C. 　　　　H. 　　　　G. 　　　　F. 　　　　E. 　　　　D.

411 I'll be able to join you.

412 I'll be able to help you.

413 I'll be able to find it.

414 I'll be able to fix it.

415 I'll be able to go with you.

416 I'll be able to be there by three.

417 I'll be able to win this time.

418 I'll be able to finish on time.

419 I'll be able to do it myself.

Study words & chunks!

⭐ Choose the correct words or chunks for each sentence and fill in the blanks. ▷

fix it

find it

finish on time

do it myself

join you

go with you

help you

win

be there

411 I'll be able to _____. (너와 함께하다)

412 I'll be able to _____. (너를 도와주다)

413 I'll be able to _____. (그것을 찾다)

414 I'll be able to _____. (그것을 고치다)

415 I'll be able to _____. (너와 함께 가다)

416 I'll be able to _____ by three. (그곳에 있다)

417 I'll be able to _____ this time. (이기다) * this time 이번

418 I'll be able to _____. (제시간에 끝내다)

419 I'll be able to _____. (그것을 스스로 하다)

Guess it!

⭐ In each picture, what would he or she most likely say?
Using 'I'll be able to ~.' make a sentence with the words or chunks below.

| be there | help you | finish on time |

| go with you | find it | win |

| do it myself | fix it | join you |

1.

_____

_____ by three.

2.

_____

_____ this time.

3.

_____

_____.

Speak Up!

⭐ Complete the dialogues with the best sentence from this track.

> **보기**
>
> A: Did you change the battery?
>
> B: I did. But it's still not working.
>
> A: Give it to me. **I'll be able to fix it**.

1

A: Let's ride bikes today.

B: But I can't ride a bike.

A: Really? 🎤 _____ ▶. I'll teach you how.   Ⓡ

2

A: Oh, I remember! I think I dropped it near the school.

B: Let's go back there.

A: Okay. 🎤 _____ ▶.   Ⓡ

3

A: Are you still working on it?

B: Yes, but 🎤 _____ ▶.   Ⓡ

A: Good. We have 10 minutes.

세이펜을 통해 각 상황에 맞는 말을 직접 녹음해 보고 확실히 익혔는지 확인해보세요.

📖 **[보기]** still 아직도 | work 작동하다 **1.** let's ~하자 | ride a bike 자전거를 타다 **2.** drop[dropped] 떨어뜨리다[떨어뜨렸다] **3.** work on ~에 노력을 들이다 | minute (시간) 분

정답과 해설 p.18

48 Track

Will you forgive me?

너는 ~할 거야? / 너는 ~해 줄래?

Say It! 1) 상대방에게 미래에 무언가를 할지 물을 때
2) 상대방에게 부탁할 때

Fill it! Listen to the track and fill in the blanks with the correct sentence number.

420 Will you wait for me?

421 Will you be there?

422 Will you go home now?

423 Will you come back soon?

424 Will you play with me?

425 Will you be on time?

426 Will you forgive me?

427 Will you keep an eye on my bag?

428 Will you stop making that noise?

Study words & chunks!

⭐ Choose the correct words or chunks for each sentence and fill in the blanks. ▷

forgive me

come back

wait for me

be there

stop making that noise

go home

keep an eye on my bag

be on time

play with me

420 Will you _____ ? (나를 기다리다)

421 Will you _____ ? (그곳에 있다)

422 Will you _____ now? (집에 가다)

423 Will you _____ soon? (돌아오다) * soon 곧

424 Will you _____ ? (나와 놀다)

425 Will you _____ ? (시간을 잘 지키다)

426 Will you _____ ? (나를 용서하다)

427 Will you _____ ? (내 가방을 지켜보다)

428 Will you _____ ? (시끄럽게 하는 것을 그만하다)

Guess it!

★ In each picture, what would he or she most likely say?
Using '**Will you ~?**' make a sentence with the words or chunks below.

stop making that noise	be on time	go home
play with me	wait for me	keep an eye on my bag
be there	come back	forgive me

1.

_____

_____ ?

Sorry..

2.

_____

_____ ?

3.

_____

_____ ?

Speak Up!

⭐ Complete the dialogues with the best sentence from this track.

> **보기**
>
> **A:** **Will you go home** now?
>
> **B:** Yes. I should go home early today.
>
> **A:** I see. See you tomorrow.
>
> *I see. 알겠어.

1

A: Let's play soccer.

B: Sure. But I have to finish this first.

🎤 _____ ▶?

*Sure. 그래.

A: Okay. Do it quickly.

Ⓡ

2

A: I need to go to the teachers' room now.

B: 🎤 _____ ▶ soon?

A: Yes. It won't take long.

Ⓡ

3

A: 🎤 _____ ▶?

I have to go to the bathroom now.

B: Okay. Put it on the desk. I can watch it for you.

Ⓡ

> 세이펜을 통해 각 상황에 맞는 말을 직접 녹음해 보고 확실히 익혔는지 확인해보세요.

📖 **1.** have to ～해야 한다 | first 먼저 | quickly 빨리 **2.** need to ～해야 한다 | teachers' room 교무실 | won't[will not] ～하지 않을 것이다 | take long (시간이) 오래 걸리다

memo

memo ✎

memo ✎

왓츠 리딩
What's Reading

쉽고 재미있게 완성되는 **영어독해력**

풍부한 읽기 경험을 쌓고, 재미있게 완성되는 영어 독해력을 확인해 보세요!

단계	단어 수	Lexile 지수	학습 대상
70 A	60 ~ 80	200-400L	영어 학습 2년차
70 B	60 ~ 80		
80 A	70 ~ 90	300-500L	영어 학습 2년차 이상
80 B	70 ~ 90		
90 A	80 ~ 110	400-600L	영어 학습 3년차
90 B	80 ~ 110		
100 A	90 ~ 120	500-700L	영어 학습 3~4년차
100 B	90 ~ 120		

* Lexile(렉사일) 지수 : 미국 교육 연구 기관 MetaMetrics에서 개발한 영어 읽기 지수로, 개인의 영어 독서 능력과 수준에 맞는 도서를 읽을 수 있도록 개발된 독서 능력 평가 지수입니다. 미국에서 가장 공신력 있는 지수로 활용되고 있습니다.

70 A | B

80 A | B

90 A | B

100 A | B

독해를 처음 시작하는 아이들을 위한
기본 독해서

문제 해결 능력을 향상시키는
심화 독해서

1
하나의 주제를 기반으로 여러 영역의 지문 제공

재미있는 픽션과 유익한 논픽션 50:50

2
독해력을 향상시키는 3단계 학습법

▸ CHECK UP 내용 확인하기
▸ BUILD UP 독해력 다지기
▸ SUM UP 지문 요약하기

3
완벽한 복습을 위한 단어 암기장과 워크북 제공

4
직독직해를 포함한 자세한 해설 제공

5
학습에 편리한 지문·어휘 MP3 파일 제공

 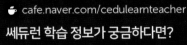

초 등 코 치

천일문
sentence

✦ ✦ ✦

WORKBOOK

with
세이펜

2

SAYPEN TV
www.saypen.com

쎄듀

천일문
sentence

✦ ✦ ✦

WORKBOOK

2

25
Track

I can ride a bike.

나는 ~할 수 있어.

Master words & chunks!

Ⓐ 상자 안에 있는 단어 조각들을 화살표로 연결하여 이번 트랙에서 배운 표현을 만들어 보세요.

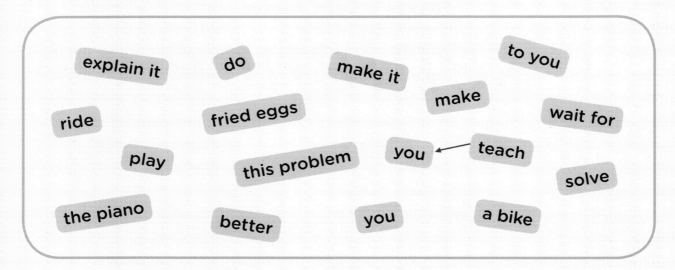

Ⓑ 상자에서 연결한 표현과 남는 단어 조각을 다시 한 번 써보고 뜻을 적어보세요.

Words & Chunks	뜻

Master sentences!

⭐ 앞에서 복습한 표현을 사용하여 이번 트랙에서 배운 문장을 각 그림에 맞게 완성해보세요.

나는 ~할 수 있어.

1 🎤   . ▷

2 🎤   . ▷

3 🎤   . ▷

4 🎤   . ▷

5 🎤   . ▷

6 🎤   . ▷

7 🎤   . ▷

8 🎤   . ▷

9 🎤   . ▷

26 Track

I can't believe it.

나는 ~할 수 없어.

Master words & chunks!

Ⓐ 상자 안에 있는 단어 조각들을 화살표로 연결하여 이번 트랙에서 배운 표현을 만들어 보세요.

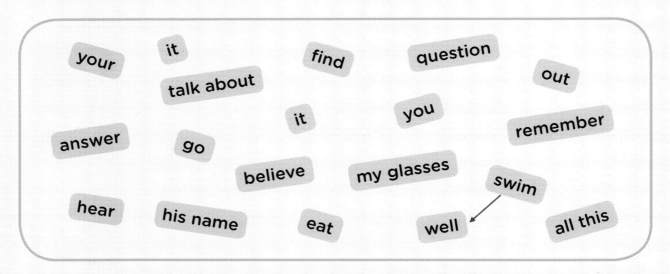

Ⓑ 상자에서 연결한 표현을 다시 한 번 써보고 뜻을 적어보세요.

Words & Chunks	뜻

Master sentences!

⭐ 앞에서 복습한 표현을 사용하여 이번 트랙에서 배운 문장을 각 그림에 맞게 완성해보세요.

나는 ~할 수 없어.

1 🎤   . ▷

2 🎤   . ▷

3 🎤   . ▷

4 🎤   . ▷

5 🎤   . ▷

6 🎤   now. ▷

7 🎤   ! ▷

8 🎤   . ▷

9 🎤   . ▷

27
Track

You can go first.

너는 ~해도 돼.

Master words & chunks!

Ⓐ 상자 안에 있는 단어 조각들을 화살표로 연결하여 이번 트랙에서 배운 표현을 만들어 보세요.

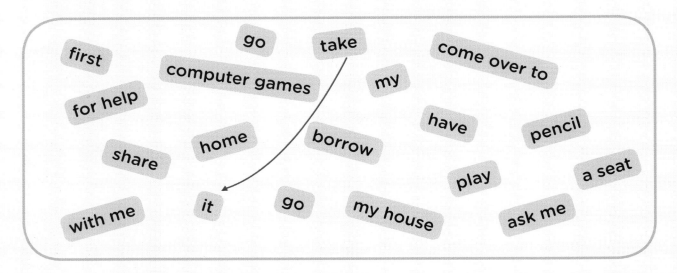

Ⓑ 상자에서 연결한 표현을 다시 한 번 써보고 뜻을 적어보세요.

Words & Chunks	뜻

Master sentences!

⭐ 앞에서 복습한 표현을 사용하여 이번 트랙에서 배운 문장을 각 그림에 맞게 완성해보세요.

너는 ~해도 돼.

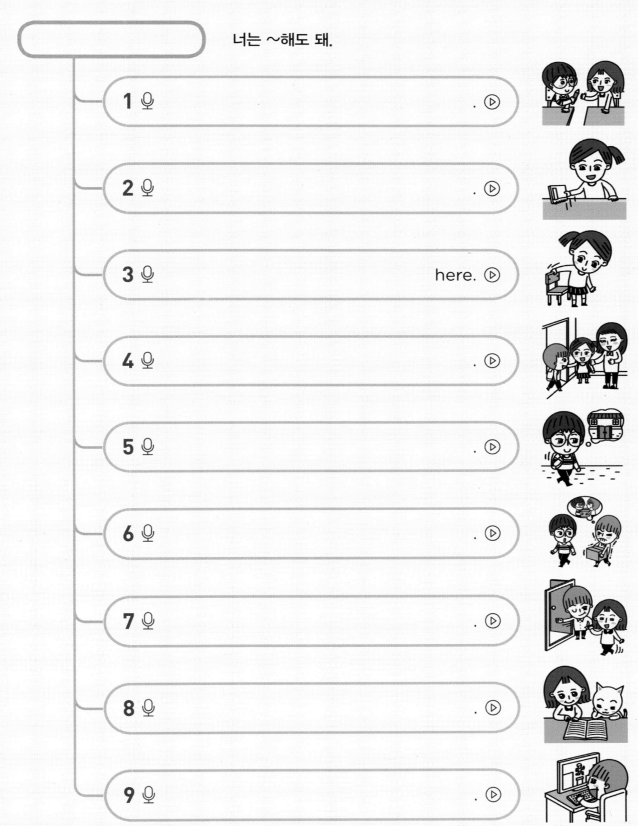

1 🎤   . ▷

2 🎤   . ▷

3 🎤   here. ▷

4 🎤   . ▷

5 🎤   . ▷

6 🎤   . ▷

7 🎤   . ▷

8 🎤   . ▷

9 🎤   . ▷

28
Track

Can I join you?

내가 ~해도 될까?

Master words & chunks!

Ⓐ 상자 안에 있는 단어 조각들을 화살표로 연결하여 이번 트랙에서 배운 표현을 만들어 보세요.

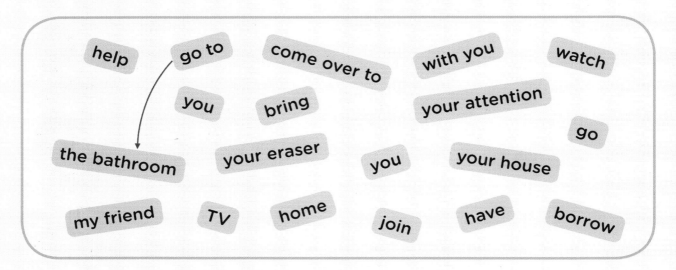

Ⓑ 상자에서 연결한 표현을 다시 한 번 써보고 뜻을 적어보세요.

Words & Chunks	뜻

Master sentences!

★ 앞에서 복습한 표현을 사용하여 이번 트랙에서 배운 문장을 각 그림에 맞게 완성해보세요.

내가 ~해도 될까?

1 🎤 _____ ? ▷

2 🎤 _____ ? ▷

3 🎤 _____ ? ▷

4 🎤 _____ ? ▷

5 🎤 _____ ? ▷

6 🎤 _____ ? ▷

7 🎤 _____ ? ▷

8 🎤 _____, please? ▷

9 🎤 _____ now? ▷

Can you tell me why?

너 ~할 수 있어? / 너 ~좀 해 줄래?

Master words & chunks!

Ⓐ 상자 안에 있는 단어 조각들을 화살표로 연결하여 이번 트랙에서 배운 표현을 만들어 보세요.

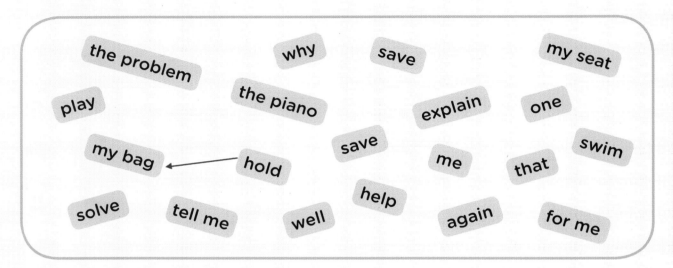

Ⓑ 상자에서 연결한 표현을 다시 한 번 써보고 뜻을 적어보세요.

Words & Chunks	뜻

Master sentences!

★ 앞에서 복습한 표현을 사용하여 이번 트랙에서 배운 문장을 각 그림에 맞게 완성해보세요.

너 ～할 수 있어? / 너 ～좀 해 줄래?

1 🎤   ? ▷

2 🎤   ? ▷

3 🎤   ? ▷

4 🎤   ? ▷

5 🎤   ? ▷

6 🎤   ? ▷

7 🎤   ? ▷

8 🎤   ? ▷

9 🎤   ? ▷

30
Track

I should get some sleep.

나[너]는 ~해야 해. / 나는 ~해야겠어.

Master words & chunks!

Ⓐ 상자 안에 있는 단어 조각들을 화살표로 연결하여 이번 트랙에서 배운 표현을 만들어 보세요.

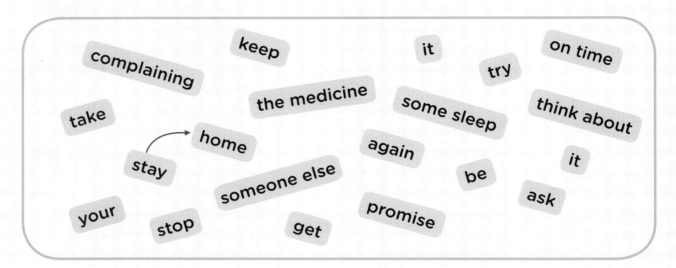

Ⓑ 상자에서 연결한 표현을 다시 한 번 써보고 뜻을 적어보세요.

Words & Chunks	뜻

Master sentences!

⭐ 앞에서 복습한 표현을 사용하여 이번 트랙에서 배운 문장을 각 그림에 맞게 완성해보세요.

나는 ~해야 해. / 나는 ~해야겠어.

1 🎤 . ▷

2 🎤 . ▷

3 🎤 . ▷

4 🎤 . ▷

너는 ~해야 해.

5 🎤 . ▷

6 🎤 . ▷

7 🎤 . ▷

8 🎤 . ▷

9 🎤 . ▷

31 Track

You must be careful.

너는 반드시 ∼해야 해.

Master words & chunks!

Ⓐ 상자 안에 있는 단어 조각들을 화살표로 연결하여 이번 트랙에서 배운 표현을 만들어 보세요.

Ⓑ 상자에서 연결한 표현을 다시 한 번 써보고 뜻을 적어보세요.

Words & Chunks	뜻

Master sentences!

앞에서 복습한 표현을 사용하여 이번 트랙에서 배운 문장을 각 그림에 맞게 완성해보세요.

너는 반드시 ~해야 해.

1   .

2   .

3   by nine o'clock.

4   every time.

5   .

6   first.

7   .

8   .

9   during the movie.

32
Track

You might be right.

나[너]는 ～일지도 몰라(～일 수도 있어).

Master words & chunks!

Ⓐ 상자 안에 있는 단어 조각들을 화살표로 연결하여 이번 트랙에서 배운 표현을 만들어 보세요.

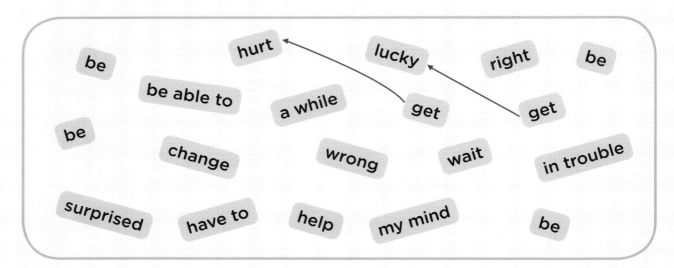

Ⓑ 상자에서 연결한 표현을 다시 한 번 써보고 뜻을 적어보세요.

Words & Chunks	뜻

Master sentences!

⭐ 앞에서 복습한 표현을 사용하여 이번 트랙에서 배운 문장을 각 그림에 맞게 완성해보세요.

나는 ～일지도 몰라(～일 수도 있어).

1 🎤 ▷ .

2 🎤 ▷ .

3 🎤 ▷ .

너는 ～일지도 몰라(～일 수도 있어).

4 🎤 ▷ .

5 🎤 ▷ .

6 🎤 ▷ .

7 🎤 ▷ .

8 🎤 ▷

9 🎤 ▷

33 Track

I have to wash my hands.

나는 ~해야 해.

Master words & chunks!

Ⓐ 상자 안에 있는 단어 조각들을 화살표로 연결하여 이번 트랙에서 배운 표현을 만들어 보세요.

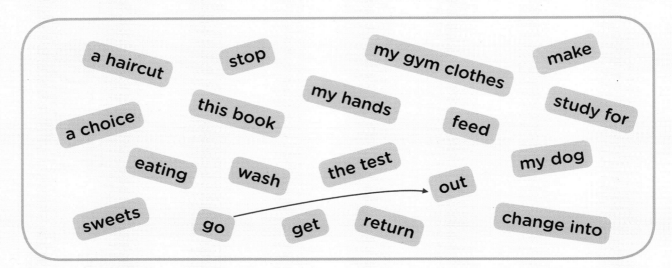

Ⓑ 상자에서 연결한 표현을 다시 한 번 써보고 뜻을 적어보세요.

Words & Chunks	뜻

Master sentences!

⭐ 앞에서 복습한 표현을 사용하여 이번 트랙에서 배운 문장을 각 그림에 맞게 완성해보세요.

나는 ～해야 해.

1 🎤   now. ▷

2 🎤   . ▷

3 🎤   . ▷

4 🎤   . ▷

5 🎤   . ▷

6 🎤   . ▷

7 🎤   tomorrow. ▷

8 🎤   . ▷

9 🎤   . ▷

34 Track

You have to see this!

너는 ~해야 해.

Master words & chunks!

Ⓐ 상자 안에 있는 단어 조각들을 화살표로 연결하여 이번 트랙에서 배운 표현을 만들어 보세요.

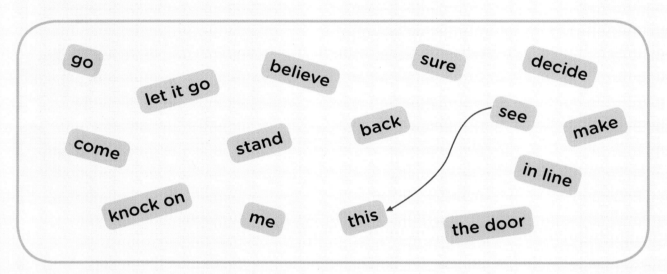

Ⓑ 상자에서 연결한 표현과 남는 단어 조각을 다시 한 번 써보고 뜻을 적어보세요.

Words & Chunks	뜻

Master sentences!

⭐ 앞에서 복습한 표현을 사용하여 이번 트랙에서 배운 문장을 각 그림에 맞게 완성해보세요.

너는 ～해야 해.

1 🎤   . ▷

2 🎤   now. ▷

3 🎤   . ▷

4 🎤   ! ▷

5 🎤   . ▷

6 🎤   now. ▷

7 🎤   . ▷

8 🎤   . ▷

9 🎤   by six. ▷

35 Track

You don't have to worry.

너는 ~할 필요가 없어(~하지 않아도 돼).

Master words & chunks!

Ⓐ 상자 안에 있는 단어 조각들을 화살표로 연결하여 이번 트랙에서 배운 표현을 만들어 보세요.

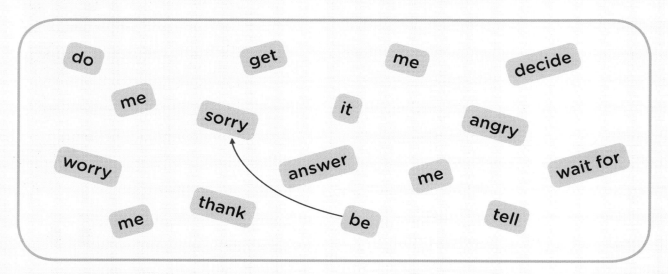

Ⓑ 상자에서 연결한 표현과 남는 단어 조각을 다시 한 번 써보고 뜻을 적어보세요.

Words & Chunks	뜻

Master sentences!

★ 앞에서 복습한 표현을 사용하여 이번 트랙에서 배운 문장을 각 그림에 맞게 완성해보세요.

너는 ~할 필요가 없어(~하지 않아도 돼).

1 🎤 . ▷

2 🎤 now. ▷

3 🎤 . ▷

4 🎤 right now. ▷

5 🎤 . ▷

6 🎤 . ▷

7 🎤 . ▷

8 🎤 . ▷

9 🎤 . ▷

36
Track

I had to stay after class.

나는 ~해야 했어.

Master words & chunks!

Ⓐ 상자 안에 있는 단어 조각들을 화살표로 연결하여 이번 트랙에서 배운 표현을 만들어 보세요.

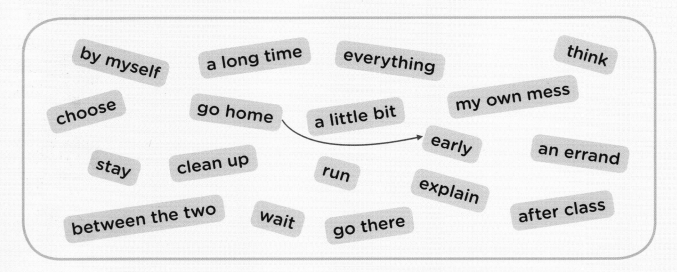

Ⓑ 상자에서 연결한 표현을 다시 한 번 써보고 뜻을 적어보세요.

Words & Chunks	뜻

Master sentences!

★ 앞에서 복습한 표현을 사용하여 이번 트랙에서 배운 문장을 각 그림에 맞게 완성해보세요.

나는 ~해야 했어.

1 🎤 .

2 🎤 .

3 🎤 .

4 🎤 .

5 🎤 .

6 🎤 .

7 🎤 .

8 🎤 .

9 🎤 .

I used to hate carrots.

나는 ~했었어(~하곤 했어).

Master words & chunks!

Ⓐ 상자 안에 있는 단어 조각들을 화살표로 연결하여 이번 트랙에서 배운 표현을 만들어 보세요.

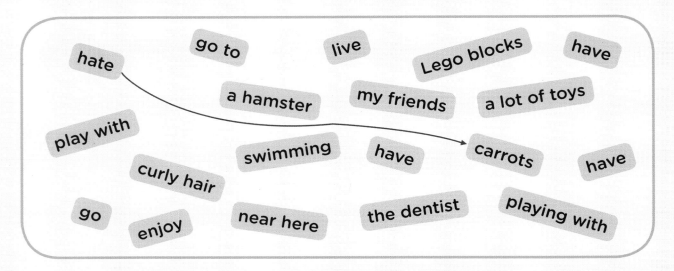

Ⓑ 상자에서 연결한 표현을 다시 한 번 써보고 뜻을 적어보세요.

Words & Chunks	뜻

Master sentences! ●——●——●——●——●——●

⭐ 앞에서 복습한 표현을 사용하여 이번 트랙에서 배운 문장을 각 그림에 맞게 완성해보세요.

나는 ～했었어(～하곤 했어).

1 🎤 . ▷

2 🎤 . ▷

3 🎤 often. ▷

4 🎤 . ▷

5 🎤 . ▷

6 🎤 here. ▷

7 🎤 . ▷

8 🎤 . ▷

9 🎤 once a week. ▷

I was disappointed.

나는 ~했어.

Master words & chunks!

Ⓐ 상자 안에 있는 단어 조각들을 화살표로 연결하여 이번 트랙에서 배운 표현을 만들어 보세요.

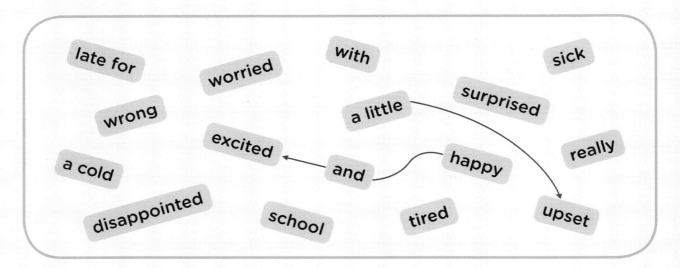

Ⓑ 상자에서 연결한 표현과 남는 단어 조각을 다시 한 번 써보고 뜻을 적어보세요.

Words & Chunks	뜻

Master sentences!

★ 앞에서 복습한 표현을 사용하여 이번 트랙에서 배운 문장을 각 그림에 맞게 완성해보세요.

나는 ~했어.

1 🎤 _____ . ▷

2 🎤 _____ . ▷

3 🎤 _____ . ▷

4 🎤 _____ . ▷

5 🎤 _____ . ▷

6 🎤 _____ . ▷

7 🎤 _____ . ▷

8 🎤 _____ . ▷

9 🎤 _____ . ▷

39
Track

He was very busy.

그[그녀]는 ~했어.

Master words & chunks!

Ⓐ 상자 안에 있는 단어 조각들을 화살표로 연결하여 이번 트랙에서 배운 표현을 만들어 보세요.

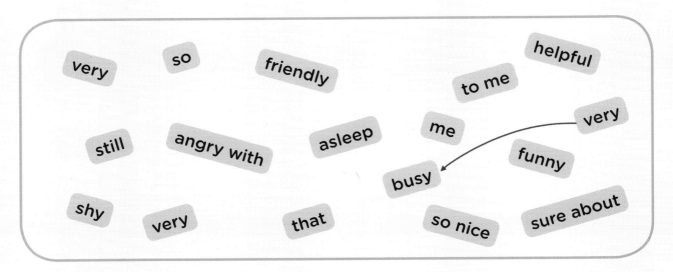

Ⓑ 상자에서 연결한 표현과 남는 단어 조각을 다시 한 번 써보고 뜻을 적어보세요.

Words & Chunks	뜻

Master sentences!

★ 앞에서 복습한 표현을 사용하여 이번 트랙에서 배운 문장을 각 그림에 맞게 완성해보세요.

그는 ~했어.

1 🎤　　　　　　　　　　　　. ▷

2 🎤　　　　　　　　　　　　. ▷

3 🎤　　　　　　　　　　　　. ▷

4 🎤　　　　　　　　　　　　. ▷

5 🎤　　　　　　　　　　　　. ▷

그녀는 ~했어.

6 🎤　　　　　　　　　　　　. ▷

7 🎤　　　　　　　　　　　　. ▷

8 🎤　　　　　　　　　　　　. ▷

9 🎤　　　　　　　　　　　　. ▷

I went to the bathroom.

나는 ~에 갔어.

Master words & chunks!

⭐ 아래 적혀 있는 한글 뜻에 알맞은 단어를 상자 안에서 찾아 완성하고, 주어진 영어 표현에는 알맞은 한글 뜻을 쓰세요.

a swimming pool   a baseball game   the library

a concert   the hospital   the classroom   the supermarket

a soccer game

the playground   the science museum   the room   the bathroom

Words & Chunks	뜻
	놀이터
bed	
the movie theater	
	과학박물관
	수영장
	슈퍼마켓
	야구 경기
	화장실
my friend's birthday party	

Master sentences!

⭐ 앞에서 복습한 표현을 사용하여 이번 트랙에서 배운 문장을 각 그림에 맞게 완성해보세요.

나는 ~에 갔어.

1 🎤 . ▷

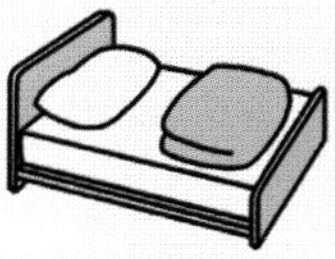

2 🎤 . ▷

3 🎤 . ▷

4 🎤 . ▷

5 🎤 . ▷

6 🎤 . ▷

7 🎤 . ▷

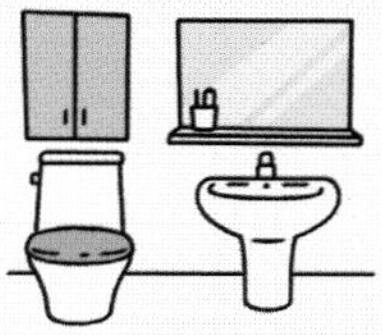

8 🎤 . ▷

9 🎤 . ▷

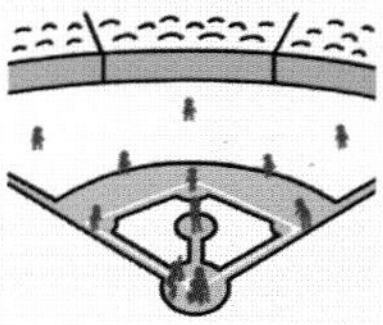

41 Track

I put it on the desk.

나는 그것을 ~에 두었어(놓았어).

Master words & chunks!

⭐ 아래 적혀 있는 한글 뜻에 알맞은 단어를 상자 안에서 찾아 완성하고, 주어진 영어 표현에는 알맞은 한글 뜻을 쓰세요.

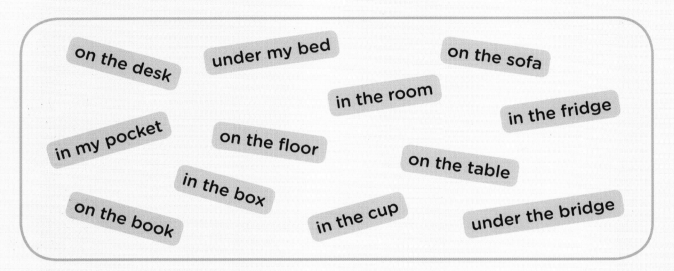

Words & Chunks	뜻
in the drawer	
	내 주머니 안에
	바닥 위에
	내 침대 밑에
	냉장고 안에
in my backpack	
	책상 위에
	테이블 위에
	상자 안에

Master sentences!

⭐ 앞에서 복습한 표현을 사용하여 이번 트랙에서 배운 문장을 각 그림에 맞게 완성해보세요.

나는 그것을 ~에 두었어(놓았어).

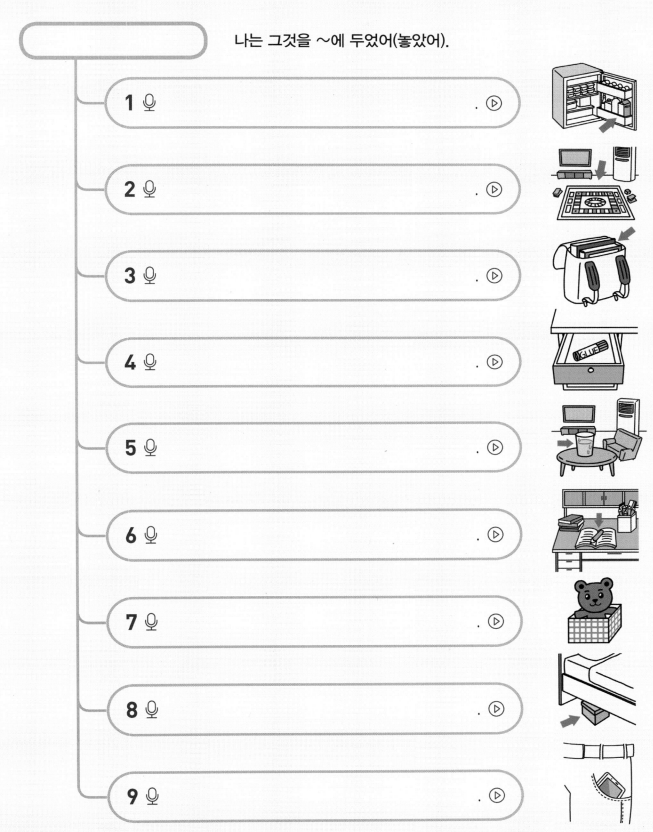

1 🎤   . ▷

2 🎤   . ▷

3 🎤   . ▷

4 🎤   . ▷

5 🎤   . ▷

6 🎤   . ▷

7 🎤   . ▷

8 🎤   . ▷

9 🎤   . ▷

42
Track

I didn't eat dinner.

나는 ~하지 않았어.

Master words & chunks!

Ⓐ 상자 안에 있는 단어 조각들을 화살표로 연결하여 이번 트랙에서 배운 표현을 만들어 보세요.

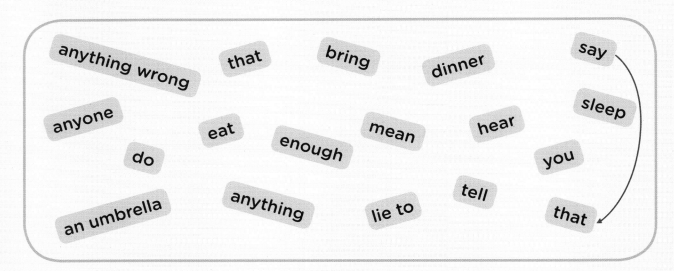

Ⓑ 상자에서 연결한 표현을 다시 한 번 써보고 뜻을 적어보세요.

Words & Chunks	뜻

Master sentences!

앞에서 복습한 표현을 사용하여 이번 트랙에서 배운 문장을 각 그림에 맞게 완성해보세요.

나는 ～하지 않았어.

43 Track

Did you get hurt?

너는 ~했어?

Master words & chunks!

Ⓐ 상자 안에 있는 단어 조각들을 화살표로 연결하여 이번 트랙에서 배운 표현을 만들어 보세요.

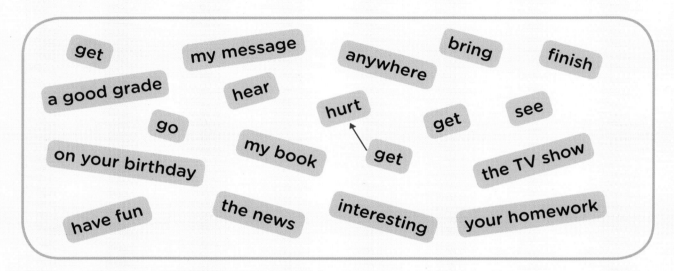

get   my message   anywhere   bring   finish

a good grade   hear   hurt   get   see

go   get

on your birthday   my book   the TV show

have fun   the news   interesting   your homework

Ⓑ 상자에서 연결한 표현을 다시 한 번 써보고 뜻을 적어보세요.

Words & Chunks	뜻

Master sentences!

⭐ 앞에서 복습한 표현을 사용하여 이번 트랙에서 배운 문장을 각 그림에 맞게 완성해보세요.

너는 ~했어?

1 🎤 ? ▶

2 🎤 ? ▶

3 🎤 ? ▶

4 🎤 ? ▶

5 🎤 ? ▶

6 🎤 ? ▶

7 🎤 ? ▶

8 🎤 ? ▶

9 🎤 ? ▶

44
Track

We will wait for you.

나[우리]는 ~할 거야(할게).

Master words & chunks!

ⓐ 상자 안에 있는 단어 조각들을 화살표로 연결하여 이번 트랙에서 배운 표현을 만들어 보세요.

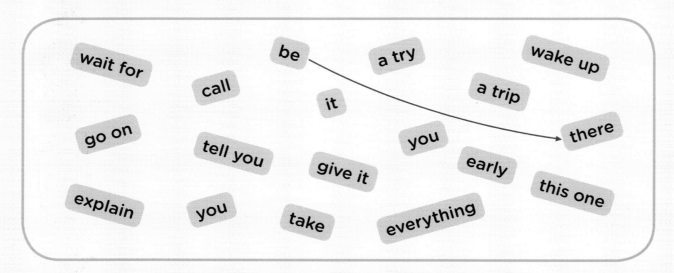

ⓑ 상자에서 연결한 표현을 다시 한 번 써보고 뜻을 적어보세요.

Words & Chunks	뜻

Master sentences!

⭐ 앞에서 복습한 표현을 사용하여 이번 트랙에서 배운 문장을 각 그림에 맞게 완성해보세요.

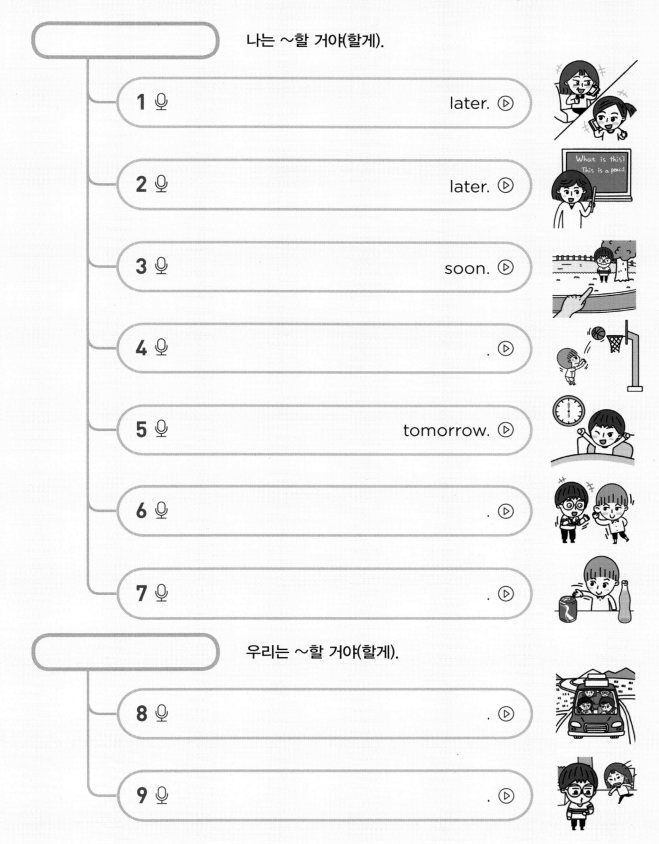

나는 ～할 거야(할게).

1 🎤   later. ▷

2 🎤   later. ▷

3 🎤   soon. ▷

4 🎤   . ▷

5 🎤   tomorrow. ▷

6 🎤   . ▷

7 🎤   . ▷

우리는 ～할 거야(할게).

8 🎤   . ▷

9 🎤   . ▷

45 Track

She will be all right.

그[그녀]는 ~할 거야.

Master words & chunks!

Ⓐ 상자 안에 있는 단어 조각들을 화살표로 연결하여 이번 트랙에서 배운 표현을 만들어 보세요.

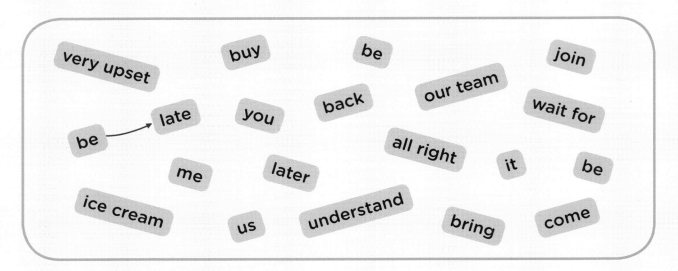

Ⓑ 상자에서 연결한 표현을 다시 한 번 써보고 뜻을 적어보세요.

Words & Chunks	뜻

Master sentences!

⭐ 앞에서 복습한 표현을 사용하여 이번 트랙에서 배운 문장을 각 그림에 맞게 완성해보세요.

그는 ~할 거야.

1 🎤   .▶

2 🎤   .▶

3 🎤   tomorrow. ▶

4 🎤   .▶

5 🎤   .▶

그녀는 ~할 거야.

6 🎤   .▶

7 🎤   .▶

8 🎤   .▶

9 🎤   .▶

46 Track

I won't tell anybody.

나는 ~하지 않을 거야(~않을게).

Master words & chunks!

Ⓐ 상자 안에 있는 단어 조각들을 화살표로 연결하여 이번 트랙에서 배운 표현을 만들어 보세요.

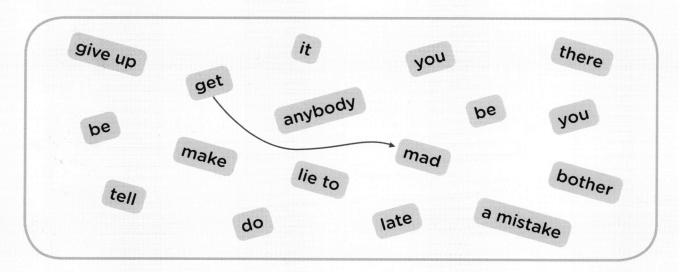

Ⓑ 상자에서 연결한 표현과 남는 단어 조각을 다시 한 번 써보고 뜻을 적어보세요.

Words & Chunks	뜻

Master sentences!

앞에서 복습한 표현을 사용하여 이번 트랙에서 배운 문장을 각 그림에 맞게 완성해보세요.

나는 ~하지 않을 거야(~않을게).

1. _____ again.

2. _____ .

3. _____ .

4. _____ .

5. _____ .

6. _____ again.

7. _____ .

8. _____ .

9. _____ .

47
Track

I'll be able to join you.

나는 ~할 수 있을 거야.

Master words & chunks!

Ⓐ 상자 안에 있는 단어 조각들을 화살표로 연결하여 이번 트랙에서 배운 표현을 만들어 보세요.

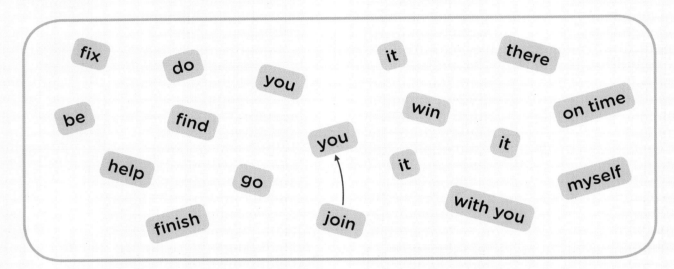

Ⓑ 상자에서 연결한 표현과 남는 단어 조각을 다시 한 번 써보고 뜻을 적어보세요.

Words & Chunks	뜻

Master sentences!

★ 앞에서 복습한 표현을 사용하여 이번 트랙에서 배운 문장을 각 그림에 맞게 완성해보세요.

나는 ~할 수 있을 거야.

1 🎙 _____ . ▷

2 🎙 _____ by three. ▷

3 🎙 _____ . ▷

4 🎙 _____ . ▷

5 🎙 _____ this time. ▷

6 🎙 _____ . ▷

7 🎙 _____ . ▷

8 🎙 _____ . ▷

9 🎙 _____ . ▷

Will you forgive me?

너는 ~할 거야? / 너는 ~해 줄래?

Master words & chunks!

Ⓐ 상자 안에 있는 단어 조각들을 화살표로 연결하여 이번 트랙에서 배운 표현을 만들어 보세요.

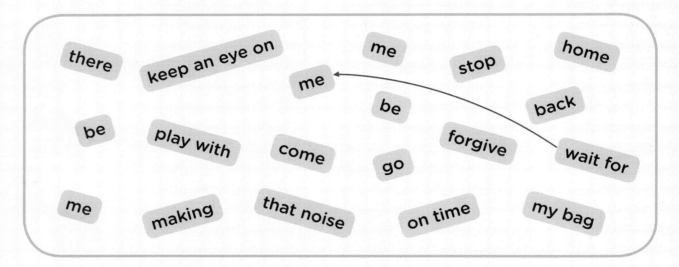

Ⓑ 상자에서 연결한 표현을 다시 한 번 써보고 뜻을 적어보세요.

Words & Chunks	뜻

Master sentences!

앞에서 복습한 표현을 사용하여 이번 트랙에서 배운 문장을 각 그림에 맞게 완성해보세요.

너는 ~할 거야? / 너는 ~해 줄래?

1   ?

2   ?

3   ?

4   soon?

5   ?

6   ?

7   ?

8   ?

9   now?

memo ☑

memo ✎

memo

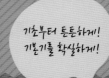

쎄듀 초·중등 커리큘럼

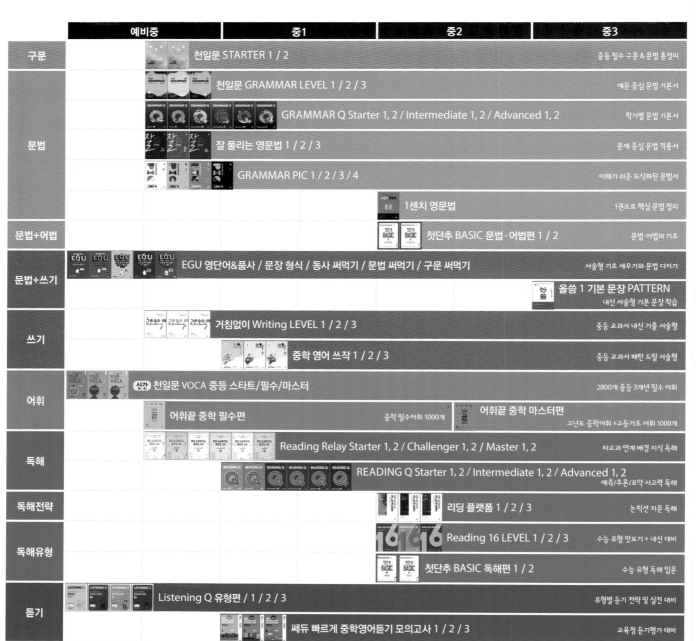

초·중등 커리큘럼 (초등)

	예비초	초1	초2	초3	초4	초5	초6
구문		신간 천일문 365 일력 |초1-3| 교육부 지정 초등 필수 영어 문장		초등코치 천일문 SENTENCE 1001개 통문장 암기로 완성하는 초등 영어의 기초			
문법				초등코치 천일문 GRAMMAR 1001개 예문으로 배우는 초등 영문법			
		왓츠 Grammar Start (초등 기초 영문법) / Plus (초등 영문법 마무리)					
독해			왓츠 리딩 70 / 80 / 90 / 100 A / B 쉽고 재미있게 완성되는 영어 독해력				
어휘			초등코치 천일문 VOCA&STORY 1001개의 초등 필수 어휘와 짧은 스토리				
		패턴으로 말하는 초등 필수 영단어 1 / 2 문장 패턴으로 완성하는 초등 필수 영단어					
ELT	Oh! My PHONICS 1 / 2 / 3 / 4 유·초등학생을 위한 첫 영어 파닉스						
		Oh! My SPEAKING 1 / 2 / 3 / 4 / 5 / 6 핵심 문장 패턴으로 더욱 쉬운 영어 말하기					
		Oh! My GRAMMAR 1 / 2 / 3 쓰기로 완성하는 첫 초등 영문법					

초·중등 커리큘럼 (중등)

	예비중	중1	중2	중3
구문		천일문 STARTER 1 / 2		중등 필수 구문 & 문법 총정리
문법		천일문 GRAMMAR LEVEL 1 / 2 / 3		예문 중심 문법 기본서
		GRAMMAR Q Starter 1, 2 / Intermediate 1, 2 / Advanced 1, 2		학기별 문법 기본서
		잘 풀리는 영문법 1 / 2 / 3		문제 중심 문법 적용서
		GRAMMAR PIC 1 / 2 / 3 / 4		이해가 쉬운 도식화된 문법서
			1센치 영문법	1권으로 핵심 문법 정리
문법+어법			첫단추 BASIC 문법·어법편 1 / 2	문법·어법의 기초
문법+쓰기	EGU 영단어&품사 / 문장 형식 / 동사 써먹기 / 문법 써먹기 / 구문 써먹기			서술형 기초 세우기와 문법 다지기
			올씀 1 기본 문장 PATTERN	내신 서술형 기본 문장 학습
쓰기	거침없이 Writing LEVEL 1 / 2 / 3			중등 교과서 내신 기출 서술형
		중학 영어 쓰작 1 / 2 / 3		중등 교과서 패턴 드릴 서술형
어휘	신간 천일문 VOCA 중등 스타트/필수/마스터			2800개 중등 3개년 필수 어휘
	어휘끝 중학 필수편 중학 필수어휘 1000개		어휘끝 중학 마스터편 고난도 중학어휘 +고등기초 어휘 1000개	
독해	Reading Relay Starter 1, 2 / Challenger 1, 2 / Master 1, 2			타교과 연계 배경 지식 독해
		READING Q Starter 1, 2 / Intermediate 1, 2 / Advanced 1, 2		예측/추론/요약 사고력 독해
독해전략		리딩 플랫폼 1 / 2 / 3		논픽션 지문 독해
독해유형		Reading 16 LEVEL 1 / 2 / 3		수능 유형 맛보기 + 내신 대비
		첫단추 BASIC 독해편 1 / 2		수능 유형 독해 입문
듣기	Listening Q 유형편 / 1 / 2 / 3			유형별 듣기 전략 및 실전 대비
		쎄듀 빠르게 중학영어듣기 모의고사 1 / 2 / 3		교육청 듣기평가 대비